101

Women

in the Bible

Bible Scriptures
&
Biblical Lessons

LOVE
GOD IS LOVE

GIL PUBLICATIONS
THE GOD IS LOVE MINISTRIES
P. O. Box 80275, Brooklyn, NY 11208
info@GILPublications.com
www.GILPublications.com

101 Women in the Bible
Bible Scriptures & Biblical Lessons

Compiled by Akili Kumasi

ISBN-13: 978-0-9626035-6-3
ISBN-10: 0-9626035-6-2

LCCN: 2008902865

Cover Art by Guy Rowe.

GIL PUBLICATIONS
THE GOD IS LOVE MINISTRIES
P. O. Box 80275, Brooklyn, NY 11208
info@GILpublications.com
www.GILpublications.com

Table of Contents

Women in the New Testament of the Bible 121

Introduction

Biblical history is full of women from all walks of life and social standing. Many made significant contributions to the Kingdom of God and some opposed the will of God.

There are heroines and villains, queens and chambermaids, aristocrats and peasants. From these women came deeds of extraordinary valor as well as conspiracies against the one true God. There were everyday hard working sacrifices and nonchalant mediocrity. No two women were the same and all have a story to be told.

While pulling together the scriptures and deciding who to include and who to not include, it became apparent that if one wanted to study the Bible it could be done effectively through the lives of these women. But also, if one wanted to study women's issues it could also be done effectively through the Bible.

This book is primarily a compilation of scriptures about those noteworthy women in the Bible. It is designed to help the researcher and the curious to find scriptures on well known women. It is not an exhaustive study as there are many, many women that are not included herein.

For exhaustive studies on women in the Bible I recommend *All the Women of the Bible* by Edith Deen and *All of the Women of the Bible* by Dr. Herbert Lockyer. Both of these books and many others on women in the Bible can be obtained from our website at www.GILpublications.com.

Akili Kumasi

The Martha Syndrome
and
the Mary Solution

Mary and Martha

God used the story of two well-known women in the Bible to demonstrate to us the type of relationship He wants with each of us.

You might remember that in one story Jesus was visiting the home of the two sisters when Martha came to Him to complain about her sister, Mary.

> **As Jesus and his disciples were on their way, he came to a village where a woman named Martha opened her home to him. She had a sister called Mary, who sat at the Lord's feet listening to what he said. But Martha was distracted by all the preparations that had to be made. She came to him and asked, "Lord, don't you care that my sister has left me to do the work by myself? Tell her to help me!"**

> **"Martha, Martha," the Lord answered, "you are worried and upset about many things, but only one thing is needed. Mary has chosen what is better, and it will not be taken away from her."**

> Luke 10:38-42 NIV

When I read this passage of scripture I get the image of a house busy with people engaged in numerous conversations around the house. Martha is running about trying to figure out how everybody is going to get fed and coordinating the logistics of cooking for all the people.

Somewhere in a secluded corner the Lord Jesus Christ is calmly teaching a handful of people who are intently listening to His every word. Mary is sitting **at His feet**, very content and very settled.

Martha frantically rushes over to interrupt the intimate gathering. Everyone casually looks up at her as the Lord easily sets the record straight. Feeling compassion for Martha, He reassuringly says, "**Martha, Martha … you are worried and upset about many things, but only one thing is needed. Mary has chosen what is better, and it will not be taken away from her.**" After all, if Jesus could feed the 4,000 (Matthew 15:32-39) and the 5,000 (Matthew 14:14-21), then certainly He could handle supper for a house full of people.

Sometimes we just forget how big our God is and we run around with what I call the "Martha Syndrome" trying to make everything just right when all we need to do is just **Trust in the Lord with all thine heart; and lean not unto thine own understanding. In all thy ways acknowledge him, and he shall direct thy paths.** (Proverbs 3:5-6 KJV)

Did not Jesus tell us to **seek ye first the kingdom of God, and his righteousness; and all these things shall be added unto you**. (Matthew 6:33 KJV) That's what Mary did. She sought Jesus first. This is what I call the "Mary Solution." But Martha was concerned about **What shall we eat? or, What shall we drink?** (Matthew 6:31 KJV)

In another story about Jesus raising Lazarus from the dead, the two sisters had different reactions to the news that Jesus was coming to see them after their brother Lazarus had died. There are many lessons that Jesus prepared us to see in this whole scenario. Herein we focus on the differences between the two sisters' approaches to Jesus before He brought Lazarus back to life.

[17]Then when Jesus came, he found that he had lain in the grave four days already.

[18]Now Bethany was nigh unto Jerusalem, about fifteen furlongs off:

[19]And many of the Jews came to Martha and Mary, to comfort them concerning their brother.

[20]Then Martha, as soon as she heard that Jesus was coming, went and met him: but Mary sat still in the house.

[21]Then said Martha unto Jesus, Lord, if thou hadst been here, my brother had not died.

[22]But I know, that even now, whatsoever thou wilt ask of God, God will give it thee.

[23]Jesus saith unto her, Thy brother shall rise again.

[24]Martha saith unto him, I know that he shall rise again in the resurrection at the last day.

[25]Jesus said unto her, I am the resurrection, and the life: he that believeth in me, though he were dead, yet shall he live:

[26]And whosoever liveth and believeth in me shall never die. Believest thou this?

[27]She saith unto him, Yea, Lord: I believe that thou art the Christ, the Son of God, which should come into the world.

[28]And when she had so said, she went her way, and called Mary her sister secretly, saying, The Master is come, and calleth for thee.

[29]As soon as she heard that, she arose quickly, and came unto him.

[30]Now Jesus was not yet come into the town, but was in that place where Martha met him.

[31]The Jews then which were with her in the house, and comforted her, when they saw Mary, that she rose up hastily and went out, followed her, saying, She goeth unto the grave to weep there.

[32]Then when Mary was come where Jesus was, and saw him, she fell down at his feet, saying unto him, Lord, if thou hadst been here, my brother had not died.

[33]When Jesus therefore saw her weeping, and the Jews also weeping which came with her, he groaned in the spirit, and was troubled.

[34]And said, Where have ye laid him? They said unto him, Lord, come and see.

[35]Jesus wept.

[36]Then said the Jews, Behold how he loved him!

[37]And some of them said, Could not this man, which opened the eyes of the blind, have caused that even this man should not have died?

[38]Jesus therefore again groaning in himself cometh to the grave. It was a cave, and a stone lay upon it.

[39]Jesus said, Take ye away the stone. Martha, the sister of him that was dead, saith unto him, Lord, by this time he stinketh: for he hath been dead four days.

[40]Jesus saith unto her, Said I not unto thee, that, if thou wouldest believe, thou shouldest see the glory of God?

John 11:17-40 KJV

Mary Got Alone With God

In verse 20 we see the first difference between Martha and Mary when they heard that Jesus **was coming**. Martha took off to go find Jesus. The King James Bible (KJV) says Mary **sat still**. Others translations say she **stayed at home** (NIV) or **remained sitting in the house** (AMP). Mary had a purpose. The Bible does not say she was crying, weeping or anxious. She was waiting on Jesus just as she had done when Jesus visited her home in the earlier example from Luke 10.

We can assume that Mary was preparing her heart through prayer. Whereas Martha was running around – the same as she had done in Luke 10.

Martha was Impatient and Anxious

In verse 25 and 26 Jesus spoke to Martha but Martha did not really hear Him (v. 21-22). She was focused on what she had to say to Him. Martha talked *at* Jesus not *to* Him and after she had her say, she left Him. The consequence was that Martha missed what Jesus was conveying to her. Do we often do the same ourselves?

Jesus must have asked Martha for Mary because when Martha got back to the house she told Mary that **The Master is come, and calleth for thee** (v. 28).

Where are We When God Calls?

Mary then went to see Jesus - at the right time. She went when He called her, once He **is come** (v. 28) or had come. She went without delay. She went when she was properly prepared because she had been praying and waiting. This is also part of the "Mary Solution," sitting and waiting on Jesus, preparing our hearts and responding appropriately when He calls.

As Mary **sat still** in her house, the Jews who were there might have thought that Mary was focused on death, sorrow, weeping, despair (v. 31). But Mary was focused on Jesus. Had she been focused solely on her brother Lazarus' death, she might have been full of unbelief and would not have been prepared to meet with Jesus.

Mary met Jesus in the same place as Martha (v. 30). She said the same thing as Martha (v. 21 and v. 32), **"Lord, if thou hadst been here, my brother had not died."** But Mary, unlike Martha, worshipped **at His feet** (v. 31) and consequently Mary got a different response. The difference was in their preparation and consequently in their approaches as well. Where we are and how we approach God makes a difference.

Both Mary and Martha were believers in the one true God, But, their walk was not the same. Mary was focused on the Savior because she had gotten quite and alone with Him. Mary met Jesus in the same place as she did when Jesus was in her home in Luke 10, **at His feet! Therefore**, Jesus was moved. **He groaned in the spirit and was troubled** (v. 33).

On the other hand, Martha had not spent the time in God's presence. Martha, just as in Luke 10 was overcome by her feelings. Her faith was not at a high level.

Our unbelief can block God's miracles in our lives. Even when Jesus was ready to raise Lazarus from the dead, Martha was filled with unbelief. She saw death. She said to Jesus, "**...Lord, by this time he stinketh: for he hath been dead four days**." This was the equivalent to Martha asking Jesus, "Why would you bother to open his grave. He's dead. He stinks. Why go there, Lord?" Martha was not ready to see the glory of God. She was not ready for God's miracle in her life.

But, again Jesus lovingly corrects the situation just as in Luke 10, when He says, "**if thou wouldest believe, thou shouldest see the glory of God**" (v. 40).

Seven Points for
Seeing God Move in Your Life

1. Wait on God by ***conditioning your heart*** (v20) through
    o   Prayer and
    o   Meditation on His Word

2. Wait on ***God's Call*** (v28)
    o   God called Mary
    o   Unlike Martha who went ahead on her own

3. Wait for ***God's Timing*** (v28)
    o   God decided when Mary should come
    o   In the meantime she was preparing herself

4. ***Listen*** for God's Call (v25-27, 28-29)
    o   God speaks to us personally

5. ***Don't delay*** when God Calls (v29)
    o   Move immediately
    o   By being prepared

6. ***Keep Focus on Him*** (v31) – Not the problem, the situation or your feelings

7. ***Worship Him at His Feet*** (v32)

Are you a Mary
Or
a Martha ... in your life with God?

Martha Syndrome	Mary Solution
Fret & Worry	Quiet
Complain	Peaceful
Focus on material surroundings	Prayerful
Anxious	At Jesus' feet
Unbelief	Faith

Biblical Lessons
on Women
From the Bible

A Virtuous Woman

Proverbs 31:10-31 KJV

Who can find a virtuous woman? for her price is far above rubies.

The heart of her husband doth safely trust in her, so that he shall have no need of spoil.

She will do him good and not evil all the days of her life.

She seeketh wool, and flax, and worketh willingly with her hands.

She is like the merchants' ships; she bringeth her food from afar.

She riseth also while it is yet night, and giveth meat to her household, and a portion to her maidens.

She considereth a field, and buyeth it:with the fruit of her hands she planteth a vineyard.

She girdeth her loins with strength, and strengtheneth her arms.

She perceiveth that her merchandise is good:her candle goeth not out by night.

She layeth her hands to the spindle, and her hands hold the distaff.

She stretcheth out her hand to the poor; yea, she reacheth forth her hands to the needy. She is not afraid of the snow for her household:for all her household are clothed with scarlet.

She maketh herself coverings of tapestry; her clothing is silk and purple. Her husband is known in the gates, when he sitteth among the elders of the land.

She maketh fine linen, and selleth it; and delivereth girdles unto the merchant.

Strength and honour are her clothing; and she shall rejoice in time to come.

She openeth her mouth with wisdom; and in her tongue is the law of kindness.

She looketh well to the ways of her household, and eateth not the bread of idleness.

Her children arise up, and call her blessed; her husband also, and he praiseth her.

Many daughters have done virtuously, but thou excellest them all.

Favour is deceitful, and beauty is vain: but a woman that feareth the LORD, she shall be praised.

Give her of the fruit of her hands; and let her own works praise her in the gates.

Proverbs: Women

v. 5:1, 18-19 KJV

...Attend unto my wisdom, and bow thine ear to my understanding:

Let thy fountain be blessed: and rejoice with the wife of thy youth.

Let her be as the loving hind and pleasant roe; let her breasts satisfy thee at all times; and be thou ravished always with her love.

v. 9:13 KJV

A foolish woman is clamorous: she is simple, and knoweth nothing.

v. 11:6 KJV

A gracious woman retaineth honour: and strong men retain riches.

v. 11:22 KJV

As a jewel of gold in a swine's snout, so is a fair woman which is without discretion.

v. 12:4 KJV

A virtuous woman is a crown to her husband: but she that maketh ashamed is as rottenness in his bones.

v. 14:1 KJV

Every wise woman buildeth her house: but the foolish plucketh it down with her hands.

of fathers: and a prudent wife is from the LORD.

v. 21:19 KJV

It is better to dwell in the wilderness, than with a contentious and an angry woman.

v. 25:24 KJV

It is better to dwell in a corner of the housetop, than with a brawling woman in a wide house.

v. 27:15 KJV

A continual dropping in a very rainy day and a contentious woman are alike.

v. 31:10, 30 KJV

Who can find a virtuous woman? for her price is far above rubies.

Favour is deceitful, and beauty is vain: but a woman that feareth the LORD, she shall be praised.

Proverbs: Wives

v. 6:29 KJV

So he that goeth in to his neighbour's wife; whosoever toucheth her shall not be innocent.

v. 18:2 NIV

He who finds a wife finds what is good and receives favor from the LORD.

v. 19:13-14 KJV

A foolish son is the calamity of his father: and the contentions of a wife are a continual dropping. House and riches are the inheritance of fathers: and a prudent wife is from the LORD.

v. 21:9 NIV

Better to live on a corner of the roof than share a house with a quarrelsome wife..

v. 21:19 NIV

Better to live in a desert than with a quarrelsome and ill-tempered wife.

v. 29:17 NIV

A quarrelsome wife is like a constant dripping on a rainy day;

Proverbs: Mothers

V 1:8 KJV

My son, hear the instruction of thy father, and forsake not the law of thy mother:

v. 10:1 KJV

The proverbs of Solomon. A wise son maketh a glad father: but a foolish son is the heaviness of his mother.

v. 15:20 KJV

A wise son maketh a glad father: but a foolish man despiseth his mother.

v. 29:15 AMP

The rod and reproof give wisdom, but a child left undisciplined brings his mother to shame.

v. 31:1 CEV

[What King Lemuel's Mother Taught Him] These are the sayings that King Lemuel of Massa was taught by his mother.

Spiritual MotherHood

Matthew 12:46-50 NIV

While Jesus was still talking to the crowd, his mother and brothers stood outside, wanting to speak to him. Someone told him, "Your mother and brothers are standing outside, wanting to speak to you."

He replied to him, "Who is my mother, and who are my brothers?" Pointing to his disciples, he said, "Here are my mother and my brothers. For whoever does the will of my Father in heaven is my brother and sister and mother."

Mark 3:31-35 NIV

Then Jesus' mother and brothers arrived. Standing outside, they sent someone in to call him. A crowd was sitting around him, and they told him, "Your mother and brothers are outside looking for you."

"Who are my mother and my brothers?" he asked.

Then he looked at those seated in a circle around him and said, "Here are my mother and my brothers! Whoever does God's will is my brother and sister and mother."

Luke 8:19-21 KJV

Then came to him *his* mother and his brethren, and could not come at him for the press. And it was told him *by* certain which said, Thy mother and thy brethren stand without, desiring to see thee. And he answered and said unto them, My mother and my brethren are these which hear the word of God, and do it.

Women in Church

2 Timothy 2:9-10 NLT

And I want women to be modest in their appearance. They should wear decent and appropriate clothing and not draw attention to themselves by the way they fix their hair or by wearing gold or pearls or expensive clothes. For women who claim to be devoted to God should make themselves attractive by the good things they do.

1 Timothy 2:11-15 KJV

Let the woman learn in silence with all subjection. But I suffer not a woman to teach, nor to usurp authority over the man, but to be in silence. For Adam was first formed, then Eve. And Adam was not deceived, but the woman being deceived was in the transgression. Notwithstanding she shall be saved in child-bearing, if they continue in faith and charity and holiness with sobriety.

1 Corinthians 14:33-35 NIV

As in all the congregations of the saints, women should remain silent in the churches. They are not allowed to speak, but must be in submission, as the Law says. If they want to inquire about something, they should ask their own husbands at home; for it is disgraceful for a woman to speak in the church.

A Woman's Beauty Is Measured By

Proverbs 31:30 KJV

Favour is deceitful, and beauty is vain: but a woman that feareth the LORD, she shall be praised.

1 Peter 3:3-5 NLT

Don't be concerned about the outward beauty that depends on fancy hairstyles, expensive jewelry, or beautiful clothes. You should be known for the beauty that comes from within, the unfading beauty of a gentle and quiet spirit, which is so precious to God. That is the way the holy women of old made themselves beautiful.

1 Timothy 2:9-10 KJV

In like manner also, that women adorn themselves in modest apparel, with shamefacedness and sobriety; not with broided hair, or gold, or pearls, or costly array; But (which becometh women professing godliness) with good works.

1 Timothy 2:9-10 NLT

And I want women to be modest in their appearance. They should wear decent and appropriate clothing and not draw attention to themselves by the way they fix their hair or by wearing gold or pearls or expensive clothes. For women who claim to be devoted to God should make themselves attractive by the good things they do.

Aged and Young Women

Titus 2:1-5 KJV

But speak thou the things which become sound doctrine: That the aged men be sober, grave, temperate, sound in faith, in charity, in patience. The aged women likewise, that *they be* in behavior as becometh holiness, not false accusers, not given to much wine, teachers of good things; That they may teach the young women to be sober, to love their husbands, to love their children, *To be* discreet, chaste, keepers at home, good, obedient to their own husbands, that the word of God be not blasphemed.

Widows and Idle Women

1 Timothy 5:1-16 KJV

Rebuke not an elder, but entreat *him* as a father; *and* the younger men as brethren; The elder women as mothers; the younger as sisters, with all purity.

Honour widows that are widows indeed. But if any widow have children or nephews, let them learn first to show piety at home, and to requite their parents: for that is good and acceptable before God. Now she that is a widow indeed, and desolate, trusteth in God, and continueth in supplications and prayers night and day.

But she that liveth in pleasure is dead while she liveth. And these things give in charge, that they may be blameless. But if any provide not for his own, and specially for those of his own house, he hath denied the faith, and is worse than an infidel.

Let not a widow be taken into the number under threescore years old, having been the wife of one man, Well reported of for good works; if she have brought up children, if she have lodged strangers, if she have washed the saints' feet, if she have relieved the afflicted, if she have diligently followed every good work.

But the younger widows refuse: for when they have begun to wax wanton against Christ, they will marry; Having damnation, because they have cast off their first faith. And withal they learn *to be* idle, wandering about from house to house; and not only idle, but tattlers also and busybodies, speaking things which they ought not.

I will therefore that the younger women marry, bear children, guide the house, give none occasion to the adversary to speak reproachfully. For some are already turned aside after Satan.

If any man or woman that believeth have widows, let them relieve them, and let not the church be charged; that it may relieve them that are widows indeed.

Godly Wives

Ephesians 5:21-22 NIV

Submit to one another out of reverence for Christ.

Wives, submit to your husbands as to the Lord. For the husband is the head of the wife as Christ is the head of the church, his body, of which he is the Savior. Now as the church submits to Christ, so also wives should submit to their husbands in everything.

Husbands, love your wives, just as Christ loved the church and gave himself up for her to make her holy, cleansing her by the washing with water through the word, and to present her to himself as a radiant church, without stain or wrinkle or any other blemish, but holy and blameless. In this same way, husbands ought to love their wives as their own bodies. He who loves his wife loves himself. After all, no one ever hated his own body, but he feeds and cares for it, just as Christ does the church—for we are members of his body. "For this reason a man will leave his father and mother and be united to his wife, and the two will become one flesh."This is a profound mystery—but I am talking about Christ and the church. However, each one of you also must love his wife as he loves himself, and the wife must respect her husband.

1 Corinthians 7:10-14a NIV

To the married I give this command (not I, but the Lord):A wife must not separate from her husband. But if she does, she must remain unmarried or else be reconciled to her husband. And a husband must not divorce his wife.

To the rest I say this (I, not the Lord):If any brother has a wife who is not a believer and she is willing to live with him, he must not divorce her. And if a woman has a husband who is not a believer and he is willing to live with her, she must not divorce him. For the unbelieving husband has been sanctified through his wife, and the unbelieving wife has been sanctified through her believing husband.

Women in the
Old Testament
of the Bible

Abijah (Abi)

2 Kings 18:1-2 KJV

Now it came to pass in the third year of Hoshea son of Elah king of Israel, that Hezekiah the son of Ahaz king of Judah began to reign.

Twenty and five years old was he when he began to reign; and he reigned twenty and nine years in Jerusalem. His mother's name also was Abi, the daughter of Zachariah.

II Chronicles 29:1 KJV

Hezekiah began to reign when he was five and twenty years old, and he reigned nine and twenty years in Jerusalem. And his mother's name was Abijah, the daughter of Zechariah.

Abishag

I Kings 1:1-4; 2:13-25 KJV

Now king David was old and stricken in years; and they covered him with clothes, but he gat no heat. Wherefore his servants said unto him, Let there be sought for my lord the king a young virgin: and let her stand before the king, and let her cherish him, and let her lie in thy bosom, that my lord the king may get heat.

So they sought for a fair damsel throughout all the coasts of Israel, and found Abishag a Shunammite, and brought her to the king.

And the damsel was very fair, and cherished the king, and ministered to him: but the king knew her not.

And Adonijah the son of Haggith came to Bathsheba the mother of Solomon. And she said, Comest thou peaceably? And he said, Peaceably.

He said moreover, I have somewhat to say unto thee. And she said, Say on.

And he said, Thou knowest that the kingdom was mine, and that all Israel set their faces on me, that I should reign: howbeit the kingdom is turned about, and is become my brother's: for it was his from the LORD.

And now I ask one petition of thee, deny me not. And she said unto him, Say on.

And he said, Speak, I pray thee, unto Solomon the king, (for he will not say thee nay,) that he give me Abishag the Shunammite to wife.

And Bathsheba said, Well; I will speak for thee unto the king. Bathsheba therefore went unto king Solomon, to speak unto him for Adonijah. And the king rose up to meet her, and bowed himself unto her, and sat down on his throne, and caused a seat to be set for the king's mother; and she sat on his right hand.

Then she said, I desire one small petition of thee; I pray thee, say me not nay. And the king said unto her, Ask on, my mother: for I will not say thee nay.

And she said, Let Abishag the Shunammite be given to Adonijah thy brother to wife.

And king Solomon answered and said unto his mother, And why dost thou ask Abishag the Shunammite for Adonijah? ask for him the kingdom also; for he is mine elder brother; even for him, and for Abiathar the priest, and for Joab the son of Zeruiah.

Then king Solomon sware by the LORD, saying, God do so to me, and more also, if Adonijah have not spoken this word against his own life.

Now therefore, as the LORD liveth, which hath established me, and set me on the throne of David my father, and who hath made me an house, as he promised, Adonijah shall be put to death this day.

And king Solomon sent by the hand of Benaiah the son of Jehoiada; and he fell upon him that he died.

Abigail

1 Samuel 25:3-5, 14, 17-19, 23-25, 32-33, 36-42 NLT

This man's name was Nabal, and his wife, Abigail, was a sensible and beautiful woman. But Nabal, a descendant of Caleb, was mean and dishonest in all his dealings.

When David heard that Nabal was shearing his sheep, he sent ten of his young men to Carmel.

Meanwhile, one of Nabal's servants went to Abigail and told her, "David sent men from the wilderness to talk to our master, and he insulted them.

You'd better think fast, for there is going to be trouble for our master and his whole family. He's so ill-tempered that no one can even talk to him!"

Abigail lost no time. She quickly gathered two hundred loaves of bread, two skins of wine, five dressed sheep, nearly a bushel of roasted grain, one hundred raisin cakes, and two hundred fig cakes. She packed them on donkeys and said to her servants,

"Go on ahead. I will follow you shortly." But she didn't tell her husband what she was doing.

When Abigail saw David, she quickly got off her donkey and bowed low before him. She fell at his feet and said, "I accept all blame in this matter, my lord. Please listen to what I have to say. I know Nabal is a wicked and ill-tempered man; please don't pay any attention to him. He is a fool, just as his name suggests. But I never even saw the messengers you sent.

David replied to Abigail, "Praise the LORD, the God of Israel, who has sent you to meet me today! Thank God for your good sense! Bless you for keeping me from murdering the man and carrying out vengeance with my own hands.

When Abigail arrived home, she found that Nabal had thrown a big party and was celebrating like a king. He was very drunk, so she didn't tell him anything about her meeting with David until the next morning. The next morning when he was sober, she told him what had happened. As a result he had a stroke, and he lay on his bed paralyzed. About ten days later, the LORD struck him and he died.

When David heard that Nabal was dead, he said, "Praise the LORD, who has paid back Nabal and kept me from doing it myself. Nabal has received the punishment for his sin." Then David wasted no time in sending messengers to Abigail to ask her to become his wife.

When the messengers arrived at Carmel, they told Abigail, "David has sent us to ask if you will marry him."

She bowed low to the ground and responded, "Yes, I am even willing to become a slave to David's servants!" Quickly getting ready, she took along five of her servant girls as attendants, mounted her donkey, and went with David's messengers. And so she became his wife.

Achsah (Caleb's Daughter)

Joshua 15:16-20 KJV

And Caleb said, He that smiteth Kirjathsepher, and taketh it, to him will I give Achsah my daughter to wife.

And Othniel the son of Kenaz, the brother of Caleb, took it: and he gave him Achsah his daughter to wife.

And it came to pass, as she came unto him, that she moved him to ask of her father a field: and she lighted off her ass; and Caleb said unto her, What wouldest thou?

Who answered, Give me a blessing; for thou hast given me a south land; give me also springs of water. And he gave her the upper springs, and the nether springs.

This is the inheritance of the tribe of the children of Judah according to their families.

Judges 1:12-15 CEV

Caleb told his troops, "The man who captures Kiriath-Sepher can marry my daughter Achsah."

Caleb's nephew Othniel captured Kiriath-Sepher, so Caleb let him marry Achsah. Othniel was the son of Caleb's younger brother Kenaz.

Right after the wedding, Achsah started telling Othniel that he ought to ask her father for a field. She went to see her father, and while she was getting down from her donkey, Caleb asked, "What's bothering you?"

She answered, "I need your help. The land you gave me is in the Southern Desert, so please give me some spring-fed ponds for a water supply."

Caleb gave her a couple of small ponds named Higher Pond and Lower Pond.

Adah and Zillah

Genesis 4:19-23 KJV

And Lamech took unto him two wives: the name of the one was Adah, and the name of the other Zillah.

And Adah bare Jabal: he was the father of such as dwell in tents, and of such as have cattle.

And his brother's name was Jubal: he was the father of all such as handle the harp and organ.

And Zillah, she also bare Tubalcain, an instructer of every artificer in brass and iron: and the sister of Tubalcain was Naamah.

And Lamech said unto his wives, Adah and Zillah, Hear my voice; ye wives of Lamech, hearken unto my speech ...

Asenath, Joseph's Wife

Genesis 41:45-50 KJV

And Pharaoh called Joseph's name Zaphnathpaaneah; and he gave him to wife Asenath the daughter of Potipherah priest of On. And Joseph went out over all the land of Egypt.

And Joseph was thirty years old when he stood before Pharaoh king of Egypt. And Joseph went out from the presence of Pharaoh, and went throughout all the land of Egypt.

And in the seven plenteous years the earth brought forth by handfuls.

And he gathered up all the food of the seven years, which were in the land of Egypt, and laid up the food in the cities: the food of the field, which was round about every city, laid he up in the same.

And Joseph gathered corn as the sand of the sea, very much, until he left numbering; for it was without number.

And unto Joseph were born two sons before the years of famine came, which Asenath the daughter of Potipherah priest of On bare unto him.

And Joseph called the name of the firstborn Manasseh: For God, said he, hath made me forget all my toil, and all my father's house.

And the name of the second called he Ephraim: For God hath caused me to be fruitful in the land of my affliction.

Athaliah & Jehosheba

II Kings 8:16-18, 26 KJV

In the fifth year of Joram son of Ahab king of Israel, Jehoshaphat being then king of Judah, Jehoram son of Jehoshaphat king of Judah began to reign.

He was thirty-two years old when he began to reign, and he reigned eight years in Jerusalem.

He walked in the ways of the kings of Israel, as did the house of Ahab, for [Athaliah] the daughter of Ahab was his wife. He did evil in the sight of the Lord.

Ahaziah was twenty-two years old when he began to reign, and he reigned one year in Jerusalem. His mother's name was Athaliah, the granddaughter of Omri king of Israel.

2 Kings 11:1-3 KJV

And when Athaliah the mother of Ahaziah saw that her son was dead, she arose and destroyed all the seed royal.

But Jehosheba, the daughter of king Joram, sister of Ahaziah, took Joash the son of Ahaziah, and stole him from among the king's sons which were slain; and they hid him, even him and his nurse, in the bedchamber from Athaliah, so that he was not slain.

And he was with her hid in the house of the LORD six years. And Athaliah did reign over the land.

II Chronicles 23:13-21 KJV

And she looked, and, behold, the king stood at his pillar at the entering in, and the princes and the trumpets by the king: and all the people of the land rejoiced, and sounded with trumpets, also the singers with instruments of musick, and such as taught to sing praise. Then Athaliah rent her clothes, and said, Treason, Treason.

Then Jehoiada the priest brought out the captains of hundreds that were set over the host, and said unto them, Have her forth of the ranges: and whoso followeth her, let him be slain with the sword. For the priest said, Slay her not in the house of the LORD.

So they laid hands on her; and when she was come to the entering of the horse gate by the king's house, they slew her there.

And Jehoiada made a covenant between him, and between all the people, and between the king, that they should be the LORD's people.

Then all the people went to the house of Baal, and brake it down, and brake his altars and his images in pieces, and slew Mattan the priest of Baal before the altars.

Also Jehoiada appointed the offices of the house of the LORD by the hand of the priests the Levites, whom David had distributed in the house of the LORD, to offer the burnt offerings of the LORD, as it is written in the law of Moses, with rejoicing and with singing, as it was ordained by David.

And he set the porters at the gates of the house of the LORD, that none which was unclean in any thing should enter in.

And he took the captains of hundreds, and the nobles, and the governors of the people, and all the people of the land, and brought down the king from the house of the LORD: and they came through the high gate into the king's house, and set the king upon the throne of the kingdom.

And all the people of the land rejoiced: and the city was quiet, after that they had slain Athaliah with the sword.

II Chronicles 23:1-15 KJV

In the seventh year Jehoiada [the priest] took strength and courage and made a covenant with the captains of hundreds: Azariah son of Jeroham, Ishmael son of Jehohanan, Azariah son of Obed, Maaseiah son of Adaiah, and Elishaphat son of Zichri.

And they went about in Judah and gathered the Levites out of all the cities, and the chiefs of the fathers' houses of Israel, and they came to Jerusalem.

And all the assembly made a covenant in the house of God with the king [little Joash, to suddenly proclaim his sovereignty and overthrow Athaliah's tyranny]. And Jehoiada the priest said to them, Behold, the king's son shall reign, as the Lord has said of the offspring of David...

And the Levites shall surround the young king, every man with his weapons in his hand; and whoever comes into the house [breaking through the ranks of the guard to get near Joash] shall be put to death. But you be with the king when he comes in [from the temple chamber where he is hiding] and when he goes out.

So the Levites and all Judah did according to all that Jehoiada the priest had commanded...

for they brought out the king's son and put the crown on him and gave him the testimony or law and made him king. And Jehoiada and his sons anointed him and said, Long live the king!

When Athaliah heard the noise of the people running and praising the king, she went into the Lord's house to the people...

Athaliah rent her clothes and cried, Treason! Treason!

Then Jehoiada the priest commanded the captains of hundreds who were over the army, Bring her out between the ranks, and whoever follows her, let him be slain with the sword. For the priest said, Do not slay her in the Lord's house.

So they made way for Athaliah, and she went into the entrance of the Horse Gate of the king's house; there they slew her.

II Chronicles 24:7

For the sons of Athaliah, that wicked woman, had broken up the house of God; and also all the dedicated things of the house of the LORD did they bestow upon Baalim.

Bathsheba

2 Samuel 11:1-5 NLT

The following spring, the time of year when kings go to war, David sent Joab and the Israelite army to destroy the Ammonites. In the process they laid siege to the city of Rabbah. But David stayed behind ...

Late one afternoon David got out of bed after taking a nap and went for a stroll on the roof of the palace. As he looked out over the city, he noticed a woman of unusual beauty taking a bath. He sent someone to find out who she was, and he was told, "She is Bathsheba, the daughter of Eliam and the wife of Uriah the Hittite." Then David sent for her; and when she came to the palace, he slept with her. (She had just completed the purification rites after having her menstrual period.) Then she returned home. Later, when Bathsheba discovered that she was pregnant, she sent a message to inform David.

2 Samuel 11:15, 26-27 KJV

And he wrote in the letter, saying, Set ye Uriah in the forefront of the hottest battle, and retire ye from him, that he may be smitten, and die ...

And when the wife of Uriah heard that Uriah her husband was dead, she mourned for her husband.

And when the mourning was past, David sent and fetched her to his house, and she became his wife, and bare him a son. But the thing that David had done displeased the LORD.

2 Samuel 12:14, 24 KJV

Howbeit, because by this deed thou hast given great occasion to the enemies of the LORD to blaspheme, the child also that is born unto thee shall surely die ... And David comforted Bathsheba his wife, and went in unto her, and lay with her: and she bare a son, and he called his name Solomon: and the LORD loved him.

1 King 1:15-21, 28-30 NIV

So Bathsheba went to see the aged king in his room ... bowed low and knelt before the king. "My lord, you yourself swore to me your servant by the LORD your God: 'Solomon your son shall be king after me, and he will sit on my throne.' But now Adonijah has become king, and you, my lord the king, do not know about it ... the eyes of all Israel are on you, to learn from you who will sit on the throne of my lord the king after him.

... The king then took an oath: "As surely as the LORD lives, who has delivered me out of every trouble, I will surely carry out today what I swore to you by the LORD, the God of Israel: Solomon your son shall be king after me, and he will sit on my throne in my place."

Bilhah

Genesis 29:28-29 KJV

A week after Jacob had married Leah, Laban gave him Rachel, too. (Laban gave Rachel a servant, Bilhah, to be her maid.)

Genesis 30:1-12 KJV

And when Rachel saw that she bare Jacob no children, Rachel envied her sister; and said unto Jacob, Give me children, or else I die.

And Jacob's anger was kindled against Rachel: and he said, Am I in God's stead, who hath withheld from thee the fruit of the womb?

And she said, Behold my maid Bilhah, go in unto her; and she shall bear upon my knees, that I may also have children by her.

And she gave him Bilhah her handmaid to wife: and Jacob went in unto her.

And Bilhah conceived, and bare Jacob a son.

And Rachel said, God hath judged me, and hath also heard my voice, and hath given me a son: therefore called she his name Dan.

And Bilhah Rachel's maid conceived again, and bare Jacob a second son.

And Rachel said, With great wrestlings have I wrestled with my sister, and I have prevailed: and she called his name Naphtali.

When Leah saw that she had left bearing, she took Zilpah her maid, and gave her Jacob to wife.

And Zilpah Leah's maid bare Jacob a son.

And Leah said, A troop cometh: and she called his name Gad.

And Zilpah Leah's maid bare Jacob a second son.

Genesis 35:22-35 KJV

And it came to pass, when Israel dwelt in that land, that Reuben went and lay with Bilhah his father's concubine: and Israel heard it. Now the sons of Jacob were twelve:

The sons of Leah; Reuben, Jacob's firstborn, and Simeon, and Levi, and Judah, and Issachar, and Zebulun:

The sons of Rachel; Joseph, and Benjamin:

And the sons of Bilhah, Rachel's handmaid; Dan, and Naphtali:

Candace

Acts 8: 26-29 KJV

And the angel of the Lord spake unto Philip, saying, Arise, and go toward the south unto the way that goeth down from Jerusalem unto Gaza, which is desert.

And he arose and went: and, behold, a man of Ethiopia, an eunuch of great authority under Candace queen of the Ethiopians, who had the charge of all her treasure, and had come to Jerusalem for to worship,

Was returning, and sitting in his chariot read Esaias the prophet.

Then the Spirit said unto Philip, Go near, and join thyself to this chariot.

Daughters of Men

Genesis 6:1-4 KJV

And it came to pass, when men began to multiply on the face of the earth, and daughters were born unto them, That the sons of God saw the daughters of men that they *were* fair; and they took them wives of all which they chose.

And the LORD said, My spirit shall not always strive with man, for that he also *is* flesh:yet his days shall be an hundred and twenty years.

There were giants in the earth in those days; and also after that, when the sons of God came in unto the daughters of men, and they bare *children* to them, the same *became* mighty men which *were* of old, men of renown.

Daughters of Zelophehad

Numbers 27:1-11 NIV

The daughters of Zelophehad son of Hepher, the son of Gilead, the son of Makir, the son of Manasseh, belonged to the clans of Manasseh son of Joseph. The names of the daughters were Mahlah, Noah, Hoglah, Milcah and Tirzah. They approached the entrance to the Tent of Meeting and stood before Moses, Eleazar the priest, the leaders and the whole assembly, and said, "Our father died in the desert. He was not among Korah's followers, who banded together against the LORD, but he died for his own sin and left no sons. Why should our father's name disappear from his clan because he had no son? Give us property among our father's relatives."

So Moses brought their case before the LORD and the LORD said to him, "What Zelophehad's daughters are saying is right. You must certainly give them property as an inheritance among their father's relatives and turn their father's inheritance over to them.

"Say to the Israelites, 'If a man dies and leaves no son, turn his inheritance over to his daughter. If he has no daughter, give his inheritance to his brothers. If he has no brothers, give his inheritance to his father's brothers. If his father had no brothers, give his inheritance to the nearest relative in his clan, that he may possess it. This is to be a legal requirement for the Israelites, as the LORD commanded Moses.'"

Deborah

Judges 4:1-10, 14; 5:1-2 KJV

And the children of Israel again did evil in the sight of the LORD, when Ehud was dead.

And the LORD sold them into the hand of Jabin king of Canaan, that reigned in Hazor; the captain of whose host was Sisera, which dwelt in Harosheth of the Gentiles.

And the children of Israel cried unto the LORD:for he had nine hundred chariots of iron; and twenty years he mightily oppressed the children of Israel.

And Deborah, a prophetess, the wife of Lapidoth, she judged Israel at that time. And she dwelt under the palm tree of Deborah between Ramah and Bethel in mount Ephraim:and the children of Israel came up to her for judgment.

And she sent and called Barak the son of Abinoam out of Kedeshnaphtali, and said unto him, Hath not the LORD God of Israel commanded, saying,

Go and draw toward mount Tabor, and take with thee ten thousand men of the children of Naphtali and of the children of Zebulun?

And I will draw unto thee to the river Kishon Sisera, the captain of Jabin's army, with his chariots and his multitude; and I will deliver him into thine hand.

And Barak said unto her, If thou wilt go with me, then I will go:but if thou wilt not go with me, then I will not go.

And she said, I will surely go with thee:notwithstanding the journey that thou takest shall not be for thine honour; for the LORD shall sell Sisera into the hand of a woman. And Deborah arose, and went with Barak to Kedesh.

And Barak called Zebulun and Naphtali to Kedesh; and he went up with ten thousand men at his feet:and Deborah went up with him.

And Deborah said unto Barak, Up; for this is the day in which the LORD hath delivered Sisera into thine hand:is not the LORD gone out before thee? So Barak went down from mount Tabor, and ten thousand men after him.

Then sang Deborah and Barak the son of Abinoam on that day, saying, Praise ye the LORD for the avenging of Israel, when the people willingly offered themselves.

Delilah

Judges 16:4-20 NIV

Some time later, he fell in love with a woman in the Valley of Sorek whose name was Delilah. The rulers of the Philistines went to her and said, "See if you can lure him into showing you the secret of his great strength and how we can overpower him so we may tie him up and subdue him. Each one of us will give you eleven hundred shekels of silver."

So Delilah said to Samson, "Tell me the secret of your great strength and how you can be tied up and subdued."

Samson answered her, "If anyone ties me with seven fresh thongs that have not been dried, I'll become as weak as any other man."

Then the rulers of the Philistines brought her seven fresh thongs that had not been dried, and she tied him with them. With men hidden in the room, she called to him, "Samson, the Philistines are upon you!" But he snapped the thongs as easily as a piece of string snaps when it comes close to a flame. So the secret of his strength was not discovered.

Then Delilah said to Samson, "You have made a fool of me; you lied to me. Come now, tell me how you can be tied."

He said, "If anyone ties me securely with new ropes that have never been used, I'll become as weak as any other man."

So Delilah took new ropes and tied him with them. Then, with men hidden in the room, she called to

him, "Samson, the Philistines are upon you!" But he
snapped the ropes off his arms as if they were threads.

Delilah then said to Samson, "Until now, you have
been making a fool of me and lying to me. Tell me
how you can be tied."

He replied, "If you weave the seven braids of my
head into the fabric on the loom and tighten it with the
pin, I'll become as weak as any other man." So while
he was sleeping, Delilah took the seven braids of his
head, wove them into the fabric and tightened it with
the pin.

Again she called to him, "Samson, the Philistines
are upon you!" He awoke from his sleep and pulled up
the pin and the loom, with the fabric.

Then she said to him, "How can you say, 'I love
you,' when you won't confide in me? This is the third
time you have made a fool of me ..." With such
nagging she prodded him day after day until he was
tired to death.

So he told her everything. "No razor has ever
been used on my head," he said, "because I have
been a Nazirite set apart to God since birth. If my head
were shaved, my strength would leave me ..."

When Delilah saw that he had told her
everything, she sent word to the rulers of the Philistines,
"Come back once more; he has told me everything."
So the rulers of the Philistines returned with the silver in
their hands. Having put him to sleep on her lap, she
called a man to shave off the seven braids of his hair,
and so began to subdue him. And his strength left him.

Dinah

Genesis 34:1-5, 11-13, 25-26 NIV

Now Dinah, the daughter Leah had borne to Jacob, went out to visit the women of the land. When Shechem son of Hamor the Hivite, the ruler of that area, saw her, he took her and violated her. His heart was drawn to Dinah daughter of Jacob, and he loved the girl and spoke tenderly to her. And Shechem said to his father Hamor, "Get me this girl as my wife."

When Jacob heard that his daughter Dinah had been defiled, his sons were in the fields with his livestock; so he kept quiet about it until they came home.

Then Shechem said to Dinah's father and brothers, "Let me find favor in your eyes, and I will give you whatever you ask. Make the price for the bride and the gift I am to bring as great as you like, and I'll pay whatever you ask me. Only give me the girl as my wife."

Because their sister Dinah had been defiled, Jacob's sons replied deceitfully as they spoke to Shechem and his father Hamor.

Simeon and Levi, Dinah's brothers, took their swords and attacked the unsuspecting city, killing every male. They put Hamor and his son Shechem to the sword and took Dinah from Shechem's house and left.

Esther

Esther 2:2, 4, 5-7, 16-17, 20, 21-23 NLT

[H]is attendants suggested, "Let us search the empire to find beautiful young virgins for the king ... who pleases you most will be made queen..." At the fortress of Susa there was a certain Jew named Mordecai ... had a beautiful and lovely young cousin, Hadassah ... (Esther) ... father and mother had died, Mordecai adopted her ... raised her as his own daughter ... the king loved her more than any of the other young women ... set the royal crown on her head and declared her queen instead of Vashti ... Esther continued to keep her nationality and family background a secret ... following Mordecai's orders...

... two of the king's eunuchs ... guards ... became angry at King Xerxes and plotted to assassinate him ... Mordecai heard about the plot and passed the information on to Queen Esther. She then told the king ... the two men were hanged on a gallows.

Esther 3:6,8a, 9 NLT

Haman approached King Xerxes, "...If it please Your Majesty, issue a decree that they [Jews] be destroyed ... I will give 375 tons of silver to ... government administrators ... the royal treasury."

Esther 4:7, 13, 15-16 NIV

Mordecai [told Esther] "Do not think that because you are in the king's house you alone of all the Jews will escape ... Esther [replied] ... "... gather together all the Jews ... in Susa ... fast for me ... for three days ... I and my maids will fast as you do. [then] I will go to the king, even though it is against the law. And if I perish, I perish."

Esther 5:4, 14 NIV

[Esther said to the king] "If it pleases the king ... together with Haman, come today to a banquet I have prepared ..." [Haman's] wife Zeresh and all his friends said to him, "Have a gallows built, seventy-five feet high, and ask the king ... to have Mordecai hanged on it. Then go with the king to the dinner and be happy." ... Haman ... had the gallows built.

Esther 6:1-2 NIV

That night the king could not sleep; so he ordered the book of the chronicles, the record of his reign, to be brought in and read to him. It was found recorded there that Mordecai had exposed Bigthana and Teresh ... who had conspired to assassinate King Xerxes.

Esther 7:3-10 NIV

Esther Then Queen Esther answered, "If I have found favor with you, O king, and if it pleases your majesty, grant me my life—this is my petition. And spare my people—this is my request. 4 For I and my people have been sold for destruction and slaughter and annihilation. If we had merely been sold as male and female slaves, I would have kept quiet, because no such distress would justify disturbing the king."

King Xerxes asked Queen Esther, "Who is he? Where is the man who has dared to do such a thing?"

Esther said, "The adversary and enemy is this vile Haman."

hen Haman was terrified before the king and queen. The king got up in a rage, left his wine and went out into the palace garden. But Haman, realizing that the king had already decided his fate, stayed behind to beg Queen Esther for his life.

Just as the king returned from the palace garden to the banquet hall, Haman was falling on the couch where Esther was reclining.

The king exclaimed, "Will he even molest the queen while she is with me in the house?"

As soon as the word left the king's mouth, they covered Haman's face. 9 Then Harbona, one of the eunuchs attending the king, said, "A gallows seventy-five feet high stands by Haman's house. He had it made for Mordecai, who spoke up to help the king."

The king said, "Hang him on it!" 10 So they hanged Haman on the gallows he had prepared for Mordecai. Then the king's fury subsided.

Esther 8:1-2 NIV

That same day King Xerxes gave Queen Esther the estate of Haman, the enemy of the Jews. And Mordecai came into the presence of the king, for Esther had told how he was related to her.

The king took off his signet ring, which he had reclaimed from Haman, and presented it to Mordecai. And Esther appointed him over Haman's estate.

Eve

Genesis 1:27-28; 2:18, 21-25; 3:1, 6-7, 16-17, 20; 4:1-2 NIV

So God created man in his own image, in the image of God he created him; male and female he created them. God blessed them and said to them, "Be fruitful and increase in number; fill the earth and subdue it.

The LORD God said, "It is not good for the man to be alone. I will make a helper suitable for him

So the LORD God caused the man to fall into a deep sleep ... he took one of the man's ribs ... made a woman from the rib ... and he brought her to the man. The man said, "This is now bone of my bones and flesh of my flesh; she shall be called 'woman, 'for she was taken out of man."

For this reason a man will leave his father and mother and be united to his wife, and they will become one flesh. The man and his wife were both naked, and they felt no shame.

Now the serpent was more crafty than any of the wild animals the LORD God had made ... When the woman saw that the fruit of the tree was good for food and pleasing to the eye, and also desirable for gaining wisdom, she took some and ate it. She also gave some to her husband, who was with her, and he ate it. Then the eyes of both of them were opened, and they realized they were naked; so they sewed fig leaves together and made coverings for themselves.

To the woman he said, "I will greatly increase your pains in childbearing; with pain you will give birth to children. Your desire will be for your husband, and he will rule over you." To Adam he said, "Because you listened to your wife and ate from the tree about which I commanded you, 'You must not eat of it,' "Cursed is the ground because of you; through painful toil you will eat of it all the days of your life.

Adam named his wife Eve, because she would become the mother of all the living.

Adam lay with his wife Eve, and she became pregnant and gave birth to Cain. She said, "With the help of the LORD I have brought forth a man." Later she gave birth to his brother Abel.

Ezekiel's Wife

Ezekiel 24:15-27 NLT

Then this message came to me from the Lord: 16 "Son of man, with one blow I will take away your dearest treasure. Yet you must not show any sorrow at her death. Do not weep; let there be no tears. Groan silently, but let there be no wailing at her grave. Do not uncover your head or take off your sandals. Do not perform the usual rituals of mourning or accept any food brought to you by consoling friends."

So I proclaimed this to the people the next morning, and in the evening my wife died. The next morning I did everything I had been told to do. Then the people asked, "What does all this mean? What are you trying to tell us?"

So I said to them, "A message came to me from the Lord, and I was told to give this message to the people of Israel. This is what the Sovereign Lord says: I will defile my Temple, the source of your security and pride, the place your heart delights in. Your sons and daughters whom you left behind in Judea will be slaughtered by the sword. Then you will do as Ezekiel has done. You will not mourn in public or console yourselves by eating the food brought by friends. Your heads will remain covered, and your sandals will not be taken off. You will not mourn or weep, but you will waste away because of your sins. You will mourn privately for all the evil you have done. Ezekiel is an example for you; you will do just as he has done. And when that time comes, you will know that I am the Lord."

Then the Lord said to me, "Son of man, on the day I take away their stronghold—their joy and glory, their heart's desire, their dearest treasure—I will also take away their sons and daughters. And on that day a survivor from Jerusalem will come to you in Babylon and tell you what has happened. And when he arrives, your voice will suddenly return so you can talk to him, and you will be a symbol for these people. Then they will know that I am the Lord."

Gomer

Hosea 1:1-11; 3:1-5 KJV

The word of the LORD that came unto Hosea, the son of Beeri, in the days of Uzziah, Jotham, Ahaz, and Hezekiah, kings of Judah, and in the days of Jeroboam the son of Joash, king of Israel.

The beginning of the word of the LORD by Hosea. And the LORD said to Hosea, Go, take unto thee a wife of whoredoms and children of whoredoms: for the land hath committed great whoredom, departing from the LORD.

So he went and took Gomer the daughter of Diblaim; which conceived, and bare him a son.

And the LORD said unto him, Call his name Jezreel; for yet a little while, and I will avenge the blood of Jezreel upon the house of Jehu, and will cause to cease the kingdom of the house of Israel.

And it shall come to pass at that day, that I will break the bow of Israel, in the valley of Jezreel.

And she conceived again, and bare a daughter. And God said unto him, Call her name Loruhamah: for I will no more have mercy upon the house of Israel; but I will utterly take them away.

But I will have mercy upon the house of Judah, and will save them by the LORD their God, and will not save them by bow, nor by sword, nor by battle, by horses, nor by horsemen.

Now when she had weaned Loruhamah, she conceived, and bare a son.

Then said God, Call his name Loammi: for ye are not my people, and I will not be your God.

Yet the number of the children of Israel shall be as the sand of the sea, which cannot be measured nor numbered; and it shall come to pass, that in the place where it was said unto them, Ye are not my people, there it shall be said unto them, Ye are the sons of the living God.

Then shall the children of Judah and the children of Israel be gathered together, and appoint themselves one head, and they shall come up out of the land: for great shall be the day of Jezreel.

Hosea 3:1-5 KJV

Then said the LORD unto me, Go yet, love a woman beloved of her friend, yet an adulteress, according to the love of the LORD toward the children of Israel, who look to other gods, and love flagons of wine.

So I bought her to me for fifteen pieces of silver, and for an homer of barley, and an half homer of barley:

And I said unto her, Thou shalt abide for me many days; thou shalt not play the harlot, and thou shalt not be for another man: so will I also be for thee.

For the children of Israel shall abide many days without a king, and without a prince, and without a sacrifice, and without an image, and without an ephod, and without teraphim:

Afterward shall the children of Israel return, and seek the LORD their God, and David their king; and shall fear the LORD and his goodness in the latter days.

Great Woman of Shunem

2 Kings 4:8-12, 14-21, 32, 35, 37 KJV

And it fell on a day, that Elisha passed to Shunem, where *was* a great woman; and she constrained him to eat bread. And *so* it was, *that* as oft as he passed by, he turned in thither to eat bread. And she said unto her husband, Behold now, I perceive that this *is* an holy man of God, which passeth by us continually. Let us make a little chamber, I pray thee, on the wall; and let us set for him there a bed, and a table, and a stool, and a candlestick:and it shall be, when he cometh to us, that he shall turn in thither.

And it fell on a day, that he came thither, and he turned into the chamber, and lay there. And he said to Gehazi his servant, Call this Shunammite. And when he had called her, she stood before him.

And he said, What then *is* to be done for her? And Gehazi answered, Verily she hath no child, and her husband is old. And he said, Call her. And when he had called her, she stood in the door. And he said, About this season, according to the time of life, thou shalt embrace a son. And she said, Nay, my lord, *thou* man of God, do not lie unto thine handmaid. And the woman conceived, and bare a son at that season that Elisha had said unto her, according to the time of life.

And when the child was grown, it fell on a day, that he went out to his father to the reapers. And he said unto his father, My head, my head. And he said to a lad, Carry him to his mother. And when he had taken him, and brought him to his mother, he sat on her knees till noon, and *then* died. And she went up, and laid him on the bed of the man of God, and shut *the door* upon him, and went out.

And when Elisha was come into the house, behold, the child was dead, *and* laid upon his bed.

Then he returned, and walked in the house to and fro; and went up, and stretched himself upon him:and the child sneezed seven times, and the child opened his eyes.

Then she went in, and fell at his feet, and bowed herself to the ground, and took up her son, and went out.

Hagar

Genesis 16:1-11 NIV

Now Sarai, Abram's wife, had borne him no children. But she had an Egyptian maidservant named Hagar; so she said to Abram, "The LORD has kept me from having children. Go, sleep with my maidservant; perhaps I can build a family through her." ...after Abram had been living in Canaan ten years, Sarai his wife took her Egyptian maidservant Hagar and gave her to her husband to be his wife. He slept with Hagar, and she conceived.

When she knew she was pregnant, she began to despise her mistress. Then Sarai said to Abram, "You are responsible for the wrong I am suffering. I put my servant in your arms, and now that she knows she is pregnant, she despises me. May the LORD judge between you and me."

"Your servant is in your hands," Abram said. "Do with her whatever you think best." Then Sarai mistreated Hagar; so she fled from her.

The angel of the LORD found Hagar near a spring in the desert; it was the spring that is beside the road to Shur. And he said, "Hagar, servant of Sarai, where have you come from, and where are you going?"

"I'm running away from my mistress Sarai," she answered.

Then the angel of the LORD told her, "Go back to your mistress and submit to her." The angel added, "I will so increase your descendants that they will be too numerous to count."

"You are now with child and you will have a son. You shall name him Ishmael, for the LORD has heard of your misery. He will be a wild donkey of a man; his hand will be against everyone and everyone's hand against him, and he will live in hostility toward all his brothers."

She gave this name to the LORD who spoke to her:"You are the God who sees me," for she said, "I have now seen the One who sees me." That is why the well was called Beer Lahai Roi; it is still there, between Kadesh and Bered.

Galatians 4:22-26 NIV

For it is written that Abraham had two sons, one by the slave woman and the other by the free woman. His son by the slave woman was born in the ordinary way; but his son by the free woman was born as the result of a promise.

These things may be taken figuratively, for the women represent two covenants. One covenant is from Mount Sinai and bears children who are to be slaves:This is Hagar. Now Hagar stands for Mount Sinai in Arabia and corresponds to the present city of Jerusalem, because she is in slavery with her children. But the Jerusalem that is above is free, and she is our mother.

Hannah

1 Samuel 1:1-12, 19-20, 24-24 KJV

Now there was a certain man of Ramathaimzophim ...his name was Elkanah ... he had two wives ... Peninnah had children, but Hannah had no children. And this man went up out of his city yearly to worship and to sacrifice unto the LORD of hosts in Shiloh ... when the time was that Elkanah offered, he gave to Peninnah his wife, and to all her sons and her daughters, portions:But unto Hannah he gave a worthy portion; for he loved Hannah:but the LORD had shut up her womb. And her adversary also provoked her sore, for to make her fret, because the LORD had shut up her womb... therefore she wept, and did not eat. Then said Elkanah her husband to her, Hannah, why weepest thou? and why eatest thou not? and why is thy heart grieved? *am* not I better to thee than ten sons?

So Hannah rose up after they had eaten in Shiloh, and ... drunk. Now Eli the priest sat upon a seat by a post of the temple of the LORD. And she *was* in bitterness of soul, and prayed unto the LORD, and wept sore. And she vowed a vow ... O LORD of hosts, if thou wilt indeed look on the affliction of thine handmaid, and remember me, and not forget thine handmaid, but wilt give unto thine handmaid a man child, then I will give him unto the LORD all the days of his life, and there shall no razor come upon his head. And it came to pass, as she continued praying before the LORD, that Eli marked her mouth.

And they rose up in the morning early, and worshipped before the LORD, and returned, and came to their house to Ramah:and Elkanah knew Hannah his wife; and the LORD remembered her. Wherefore it came to pass, when the time was come about after Hannah had conceived, that she bare a son, and called his name Samuel, *saying*, Because I have asked him of the LORD ...

And when she had weaned him, she took him up with her, with three bullocks, and one ephah of flour, and a bottle of wine, and brought him unto the house of the LORD in Shiloh: and the child *was* young. And they slew a bullock, and brought the child to Eli. And she said, Oh my lord, *as* thy soul liveth, my lord, I *am* the woman that stood by thee here, praying unto the LORD. For this child I prayed; and the LORD hath given me my petition which I asked of him: Therefore also I have lent him to the LORD; as long as he liveth he shall be lent to the LORD. And he worshipped the LORD there.

1 Samuel 2:1-2, 21 KJV

And Hannah prayed, and said, My heart rejoiceth in the LORD, mine horn is exalted in the LORD: my mouth is enlarged over mine enemies; because I rejoice in thy salvation. *There is* none holy as the LORD:f or *there is* none beside thee: neither *is there* any rock like our God.

And the LORD visited Hannah ... she conceived, and bare three sons and two daughters ... Samuel grew before the LORD.

Huldah

II Chronicles 34:22-33 KJV (Also: II Kings 22:14-20)

And Hilkiah, and they that the king had appointed, went to Huldah the prophetess, the wife of Shallum the son of Tikvath, the son of Hasrah, keeper of the wardrobe; (now she dwelt in Jerusalem in the college:) and they spake to her to that effect.

And she answered them, Thus saith the LORD God of Israel, Tell ye the man that sent you to me,

Thus saith the LORD, Behold, I will bring evil upon this place, and upon the inhabitants thereof, even all the curses that are written in the book which they have read before the king of Judah:

Because they have forsaken me, and have burned incense unto other gods, that they might provoke me to anger with all the works of their hands; therefore my wrath shall be poured out upon this place, and shall not be quenched.

And as for the king of Judah, who sent you to enquire of the LORD, so shall ye say unto him, Thus saith the LORD God of Israel concerning the words which thou hast heard;

Because thine heart was tender, and thou didst humble thyself before God, when thou heardest his words against this place, and against the inhabitants thereof, and humbledst thyself before me, and didst rend thy clothes, and weep before me; I have even heard thee also, saith the LORD.

Behold, I will gather thee to thy fathers, and thou shalt be gathered to thy grave in peace, neither shall thine eyes see all the evil that I will bring upon this place, and upon the inhabitants of the same. So they brought the king word again.

Then the king sent and gathered together all the elders of Judah and Jerusalem.

And the king went up into the house of the LORD, and all the men of Judah, and the inhabitants of Jerusalem, and the priests, and the Levites, and all the people, great and small: and he read in their ears all the words of the book of the covenant that was found in the house of the LORD.

And the king stood in his place, and made a covenant before the LORD, to walk after the LORD, and to keep his commandments, and his testimonies, and his statutes, with all his heart, and with all his soul, to perform the words of the covenant which are written in this book.

And he caused all that were present in Jerusalem and Benjamin to stand to it. And the inhabitants of Jerusalem did according to the covenant of God, the God of their fathers.

And Josiah took away all the abominations out of all the countries that pertained to the children of Israel, and made all that were present in Israel to serve, even to serve the LORD their God. And all his days they departed not from following the LORD, the God of their fathers.

Jael

Judges 4:17-22; 5:24-27 NIV

Sisera, however, fled on foot to the tent of Jael, the wife of Heber the Kenite, because there were friendly relations between Jabin king of Hazor and the clan of Heber the Kenite.

Jael went out to meet Sisera and said to him, "Come, my lord, come right in. Don't be afraid." So he entered her tent, and she put a covering over him.

"I'm thirsty," he said. "Please give me some water." She opened a skin of milk, gave him a drink, and covered him up.

"Stand in the doorway of the tent," he told her. "If someone comes by and asks you, 'Is anyone here?' say 'No.'"

But Jael, Heber's wife, picked up a tent peg and a hammer and went quietly to him while he lay fast asleep, exhausted. She drove the peg through his temple into the ground, and he died.

Barak came by in pursuit of Sisera, and Jael went out to meet him. "Come," she said, "I will show you the man you're looking for." So he went in with her, and there lay Sisera with the tent peg through his temple—dead.

> "Most blessed of women be Jael,
>   the wife of Heber the Kenite,
>   most blessed of tent-dwelling women.
>
> He asked for water, and she gave him milk;
>
>   in a bowl fit for nobles she brought him
>   curdled milk.
>
> Her hand reached for the tent peg,
>   her right hand for the workman's hammer.
>   She struck Sisera, she crushed his head,
>   she shattered and pierced his temple.
>
> At her feet he sank,
>   he fell; there he lay.
>   At her feet he sank, he fell;
>   where he sank, there he fell—dead.

Jephthah's Daughter

Judges 11:30-40 KJV

And Jephthah vowed a vow unto the LORD, and said, If thou shalt without fail deliver the children of Ammon into mine hands, Then it shall be, that whatsoever cometh forth of the doors of my house to meet me, when I return in peace from the children of Ammon, shall surely be the LORD'S, and I will offer it up for a burnt offering.

So Jephthah passed over unto the children of Ammon to fight against them; and the LORD delivered them into his hands. And he smote them from Aroer, even till thou come to Minnith, *even* twenty cities, and unto the plain of the vineyards, with a very great slaughter. Thus the children of Ammon were subdued before the children of Israel.

And Jephthah came to Mizpeh unto his house, and, behold, his daughter came out to meet him with timbrels and with dances: and she *was his* only child; beside her he had neither son nor daughter. And it came to pass, when he saw her, that he rent his clothes, and said, Alas, my daughter! thou hast brought me very low, and thou art one of them that trouble me: for I have opened my mouth unto the LORD, and I cannot go back.

And she said unto him, My father, *if* thou hast opened thy mouth unto the LORD, do to me according to that which hath proceeded out of thy mouth; forasmuch as the LORD hath taken vengeance for thee of thine enemies, *even* of the children of Ammon. And she said unto her father, Let this thing be done for me:let me alone two months, that I may go up and down upon the mountains, and bewail my virginity, I and my fellows.

And he said, Go. And he sent her away *for* two months:and she went with her companions, and bewailed her virginity upon the mountains. And it came to pass at the end of two months, that she returned unto her father, who did with her *according* to his vow which he had vowed:and she knew no man. And it was a custom in Israel, *That* the daughters of Israel went yearly to lament the daughter of Jephthah the Gileadite four days in a year.

Jezebel

1 Kings 16:30-31 NLT

Ahab son of Omri did more evil in the eyes of the LORD than any of those before him. He not only considered it trivial to commit the sins of Jeroboam son of Nebat, but he also married Jezebel daughter of Ethbaal king of the Sidonians, and began to serve Baal and worship him.

1 Kings 18:2-4 NLT

Meanwhile, the famine had become very severe in Samaria. So Ahab summoned Obadiah, who was in charge of the palace. (Now Obadiah was a devoted follower of the LORD. Once when Jezebel had tried to kill all the LORD'S prophets, Obadiah had hidden one hundred of them in two caves. He had put fifty prophets in each cave and had supplied them with food and water.

1 Kings 19:1-3 NIV

Now Ahab told Jezebel everything Elijah had done and how he had killed all the prophets with the sword. So Jezebel sent a messenger to Elijah to say, "May the gods deal with me, be it ever so severely, if by this time tomorrow I do not make your life like that of one of them." Elijah was afraid and ran for his life.

1 Kings 21:1-11 KJV

... after these things ... Naboth the Jezreelite had a vineyard, which *was* in Jezreel, hard by the palace of Ahab ... Ahab spake unto Naboth, saying, Give me thy vineyard, that I may have it for a garden of herbs, ... Naboth said to Ahab, The LORD forbid it me, that I should give the inheritance of my fathers unto thee. And Ahab came into his house heavy and displeased ... But Jezebel his wife came to him, and said unto him, Why is thy spirit so sad, that thou eatest no bread ... Dost thou now govern the kingdom of Israel? ... I will give thee the vineyard ... she wrote letters in Ahab's name ... unto the elders and to the nobles ... saying, Proclaim a fast, and set Naboth on high among the people:And set two men, sons of Belial, before him, to bear witness against him, saying, Thou didst blaspheme God and the king. And *then* carry him out, and stone him, that he may die ... And the men of his city ... did as Jezebel had sent unto them

2 Kings 9:6-10 NLT

"This is what the LORD, the God of Israel, says ... I will avenge the murder of my prophets and all the LORD'S servants who were killed by Jezebel. The entire family of Ahab must be wiped out ... Dogs will eat

Ahab's wife, Jezebel, at the plot of land in Jezreel, and no one will bury her.

Jochebed, Moses' Mother

Numbers 26:59 KJV

And the name of Amram's wife *was* Jochebed, the daughter of Levi, whom *her mother* bare to Levi in Egypt:and she bare unto Amram Aaron and Moses, and Miriam their sister.

Exodus 2:1-20 KJV

And there went a man of the house of Levi, and took *to wife* a daughter of Levi. And the woman conceived, and bare a son:and when she saw him that he was a goodly child, she hid him three months. And when she could not longer hide him, she took for him an ark of bulrushes, and daubed it with slime and with pitch, and put the child therein; and she laid it in the flags by the river's brink. And his sister stood afar off, to wit what would be done to him.

And the daughter of Pharaoh came down to wash *herself* at the river; and her maidens walked along by the river's side; and when she saw the ark among the flags, she sent her maid to fetch it. And when she had opened *it*, she saw the child:and, behold, the babe wept. And she had compassion on him, and said, This *is one* of the Hebrews' children. Then said his sister to Pharaoh's daughter, Shall I go and call to thee a nurse of the Hebrew women, that she may nurse the child for thee? And Pharaoh's daughter said to her, Go. And the maid went and called the child's mother. And Pharaoh's daughter said unto her, Take this child away, and nurse it for me, and I will give *thee* thy wages. And the woman took the child, and nursed it. And the child grew, and she brought him unto Pharaoh's daughter, and he became her son. And she called his name Moses:and she said, Because I drew him out of the water.

Keturah

Genesis 25:1-6

Then again Abraham took a wife, and her name was Keturah.

And she bare him Zimran, and Jokshan, and Medan, and Midian, and Ishbak, and Shuah.

And Jokshan begat Sheba, and Dedan. And the sons of Dedan were Asshurim, and Letushim, and Leummim.

And the sons of Midian; Ephah, and Epher, and Hanoch, and Abidah, and Eldaah. All these were the children of Keturah.

And Abraham gave all that he had unto Isaac.

But unto the sons of the concubines, which Abraham had, Abraham gave gifts, and sent them away from Isaac his son, while he yet lived, eastward, unto the east country.

I Chronicles 1:32, 33 KJV

Now the sons of Keturah, Abraham's concubine: she bare Zimran, and Jokshan, and Medan, and

Midian, and Ishbak, and Shuah. And the sons of Jokshan; Sheba, and Dedan.

And the sons of Midian; Ephah, and Epher, and Henoch, and Abida, and Eldaah. All these are the sons of Keturah.

King Lemuel's Mother

Proverbs 31:1-9 CEV

These are the sayings that King Lemuel of Massa was taught by his mother.

My son Lemuel, you were born in answer to my prayers, so listen carefully.

> Don't waste your life
> chasing after women!
> This has ruined many kings.
> Kings and leaders
> should not get drunk
> or even want to drink.
> Drinking makes you forget
> your responsibilities,
> and you mistreat the poor.
> Beer and wine are only
> for the dying
> or for those
> who have lost all hope.
> Let them drink
> and forget
> how poor and miserable
> they feel.
> But you must defend

those who are helpless
and have no hope.
Be fair and give justice
to the poor and homeless.

Leah

Genesis 29:16-18, 20, 23, 25, 30-31, 32, 33, 34, 35; 30:11-13, 15, 18, 20-21 KJV

And Laban had two daughters ... the elder *was* Leah, and ... younger *was* Rachel. Leah *was* tender eyed; but Rachel was beautiful and well favoured. And Jacob loved Rachel; and said, I will serve thee seven years for Rachel thy younger daughter ...

And Jacob served seven years for Rachel; and they seemed unto him *but* a few days, for the love he had to her...And it came to pass in the evening, that he took Leah his daughter, and brought her to him; and he went in unto her ... And it came to pass, that in the morning, behold, it *was* Leah:and he said to Laban, What *is* this thou hast done unto me? did not I serve with thee for Rachel? wherefore then hast thou beguiled me?

And he went in also unto Rachel, and he loved also Rachel more than Leah, and served with him yet seven other years.   And when the LORD saw that Leah *was* hated, he opened her womb:but Rachel *was* barren ...

And Leah conceived, and bare a son, and she called his name Reuben:for she said, Surely the LORD hath looked upon my affliction; now therefore my husband will love me...

And she conceived again ... Simeon ... Levi ... Judah ...

And Leah said, A troop cometh:... Gad. And Zilpah Leah's maid bare Jacob a second son. And Leah said, Happy am I, for the daughters will call me blessed:and she called his name Asher.

And she said unto her [Rachel], *Is it* a small matter that thou hast taken my husband? and wouldest thou take away my son's mandrakes also? And Rachel said, Therefore he shall lie with thee to night for thy son's mandrakes ...

... Issachar ... Then she [Leah] became pregnant again and had a sixth son. She named him Zebulun, for she said, "God has given me good gifts for my husband. Now he will honor me, for I have given him six sons." Later she gave birth to a daughter and named her Dinah....

Lot's Wife

Genesis 19:12-27 NLT

At dawn the next morning the angels became insistent. "Hurry," they said to Lot. "Take your wife and your two daughters who are here. Get out of here right now, or you will be caught in the destruction of the city."

When Lot still hesitated, the angels seized his hand and the hands of his wife and two daughters and rushed them to safety outside the city, for the LORD was merciful. "Run for your lives!" the angels warned. "Do not stop anywhere in the valley. And don't look back! Escape to the mountains, or you will die."

"Oh no, my lords, please," Lot begged ... I cannot go to the mountains. Disaster would catch up to me there, and I would soon die. See, there is a small village nearby. Please let me go there instead; don't you see how small it is? Then my life will be saved."

"All right," the angel said, "I will grant your request. I will not destroy that little village. But hurry! For I can do nothing until you are there." From that time on, that village was known as Zoar.

The sun was rising as Lot reached the village. Then the LORD rained down fire and burning sulfur from the heavens on Sodom and Gomorrah. He utterly destroyed them, along with the other cities and villages of the plain, eliminating all life--people, plants, and animals alike. But Lot's wife looked back as she was following along behind him, and she became a pillar of salt.

Lot's Two Daughters

Genesis 19:30-37 NLT

Afterward Lot left Zoar because he was afraid of the people there, and he went to live in a cave in the mountains with his two daughters. One day the older daughter said to her sister, "There isn't a man anywhere in this entire area for us to marry. And our father will soon be too old to have children. Come, let's get him drunk with wine, and then we will sleep with him. That way we will preserve our family line through our father."

So that night they got him drunk, and the older daughter went in and slept with her father ...the younger daughter went in and slept with him. As before, he was unaware of her lying down or getting up again. So both of Lot's daughters became pregnant by their father.

When the older daughter gave birth to a son, she named him Moab. He became the ancestor of the nation now known as the Moabites. When the younger daughter gave birth to a son, she named him Ben-ammi. He became the ancestor of the nation now known as the Ammonites.

Maid of Naaman's Wife

2 Kings 5:1-9, 14-15 KJV

Now Naaman, captain of the host of the king of Syria, was a great man with his master, and honourable, because by him the LORD had given deliverance unto Syria:he was also a mighty man in valour, but he was a leper. And the Syrians had gone out by companies, and had brought away captive out of the land of Israel a little maid; and she waited on Naaman's wife. And she said unto her mistress, Would God my lord were with the prophet that is in Samaria! for he would recover him of his leprosy. And one went in, and told his lord, saying, Thus and thus said the maid that is of the land of Israel.

And the king of Syria said, Go to, go, and I will send a letter unto the king of Israel. And he departed, and took with him ten talents of silver, and six thousand pieces of gold, and ten changes of raiment. And he brought the letter to the king of Israel, saying, Now when this letter is come unto thee, behold, I have therewith sent Naaman my servant to thee, that thou mayest recover him of his leprosy. And it came to pass, when the king of Israel had read the letter, that he rent his clothes, and said, Am I God, to kill and to make alive, that this man doth send unto me to recover a man of his leprosy? wherefore consider, I pray you, and see how he seeketh a quarrel against me.

And it was so, when Elisha the man of God had heard that the king of Israel had rent his clothes, that he sent to the king, saying, Wherefore hast thou rent thy clothes? let him come now to me, and he shall know that there is a prophet in Israel.

So Naaman came with his horses and with his chariot, and stood at the door of the house of Elisha.

Then went he down, and dipped himself seven times in Jordan, according to the saying of the man of God: and his flesh came again like unto the flesh of a little child, and he was clean.

And he returned to the man of God, he and all his company, and came, and stood before him and he said, Behold, now I know that there is no God in all the earth, but in Israel: now therefore, I pray thee, take a blessing of thy servant.

Michal

1 Samuel 14:49; 18:19-21, 25-29; 19:11-13, 17; 25:42-44 KJV

Now the sons of Saul were Jonathan, and Ishui, and Melchishua:and the names of his two daughters *were these*; the name of the firstborn Merab, and the name of the younger Michal...

But it came to pass at the time when Merab Saul's daughter should have been given to David, that she was given unto Adriel the Meholathite to wife. And Michal Saul's daughter loved David:and they told Saul, and the thing pleased him. And Saul said, I will give him her, that she may be a snare to him, and that the hand of the Philistines may be against him. Wherefore Saul said to David, Thou shalt this day be my son in law in *the one of* the twain.

And Saul said, Thus shall ye say to David, The king desireth not any dowry, but an hundred foreskins of the Philistines, to be avenged of the king's enemies. But Saul thought to make David fall by the hand of the Philistines. And when his servants told David these words, it pleased David well to be the king's son in law:and the days were not expired. Wherefore David arose and went, he and his men, and slew of the Philistines two hundred men ... Saul gave him Michal ... Saul saw and knew that the LORD *was* with David, and *that* Michal ... loved him. And Saul was yet the more afraid of David; and Saul became David's enemy continually.

Saul also sent messengers unto David's house, to watch him, and to slay him in the morning:and Michal David's wife told him, saying, If thou save not thy life to night, to morrow thou shalt be slain. So Michal let David down through a window:and he went, and fled, and escaped. And Michal took an image, and laid *it* in the bed, and put a pillow of goats' *hair* for his bolster, and covered *it* with a cloth... And Saul said unto Michal, Why hast thou deceived me so, and sent away mine enemy ...

And Abigail hasted, and arose, and rode upon an ass, with five damsels of hers that went after her;

and she went after the messengers of David, and became his wife. David also took Ahinoam of Jezreel; and they were also both of them his wives. But Saul had given Michal his daughter, David's wife, to Phalti the son of Laish, which was of Gallim.

2 Samuel 3:14; 6:15-16, 23 KJV

And David sent messengers to Ishbosheth Saul's son, saying, Deliver me my wife Michal, which I espoused to me for an hundred foreskins ...

So David and all the house of Israel brought up the ark of the LORD with shouting, and with the sound of the trumpet. And as the ark of the LORD came into the city of David, Michal Saul's daughter looked through a window, and saw king David leaping and dancing before the LORD; and she despised him in her heart ...Therefore Michal the daughter of Saul had no child unto the day of her death.

Miriam

Numbers 26:59 NLT

... Amram's wife was named Jochebed ... a descendant of Levi ... in the land of Egypt. Amram and Jochebed became the parents of Aaron, Moses, and their sister, Miriam.

Exodus 2:3-8 NLT

... when she [Moses' mother] could hide him no longer, she ... placed the child in it [basket] and put it among the reeds along the bank of the Nile. His sister stood at a distance to see what would happen to him

... Pharaoh's daughter went down to the Nile to bathe ... She saw the basket among the reeds and sent her slave girl to get it ... Then his sister asked Pharaoh's daughter, "Shall I go and get one of the Hebrew women to nurse the baby for you?" "Yes, go," she answered. And the girl went and got the baby's mother.

Exodus 14:29, 31 NIV

... Israelites went through the sea on dry ground, with a wall of water on their right and on their left ... when the Israelites saw the great power the LORD displayed ... the people feared the LORD and put their trust in him and in Moses his servant.

Exodus 15:20-21 NIV

Then Miriam the prophetess, Aaron's sister, took a tambourine in her hand, and all the women followed her, with tambourines and dancing. Miriam sang to them:

> "Sing to the LORD,
> for he is highly exalted.
> The horse and its rider
> he has hurled into the sea."

Numbers 12:1-2 KJV

... Miriam and Aaron spake against Moses because of the Ethiopian woman whom he had married ... Hath the LORD indeed spoken only by Moses? hath he not spoken also by us?

Numbers 12:4-8 NIV

At once the LORD said to Moses, Aaron and Miriam, "Come out to the Tent of Meeting, all three of you." ... Then the LORD came down in a pillar of cloud; he stood at the entrance to the Tent ... When both of them stepped forward, he said, "Listen to my words:

"When a prophet of the LORD is among you, I reveal myself to him in visions, I speak to him in dreams. But this is not true of my servant Moses; he is faithful in all my house. With him I speak face to face, clearly and not in riddles; he sees the form of the LORD. Why then were you not afraid to speak against my servant Moses?"

Naomi

Ruth 1:1-8, 14, 19-22; 2:1, 11, 20; 3:1, 13, 16-17 NIV

In the days when the judges ruled, there was a famine in the land, and a man from Bethlehem in Judah, together with his wife and two sons, went to live for a while in the country of Moab. The man's name was Elimelech, his wife's name Naomi, and the names of his two sons were Mahlon and Kilion. They were Ephrathites from Bethlehem, Judah. And they went to Moab and lived there. Now Elimelech, Naomi's husband, died, and she was left with her two sons. 4They married Moabite women, one named Orpah and the other Ruth. After they had lived there about ten years, both Mahlon and Kilion also died, and Naomi was left without her two sons and her husband...

When she heard in Moab that the LORD had come to the aid of his people by providing food for them, Naomi and her daughters-in-law prepared to return home from there. Then Naomi said to her two daughters-in-law, "Go back, each of you, to your mother's home. May the LORD show kindness to you, as you have shown to your dead and to me...

At this they wept again. Then Orpah kissed her mother-in-law good-by, but Ruth clung to her ... So the two women went on until they came to Bethlehem. When they arrived in Bethlehem, the whole town was stirred because of them, and the women exclaimed, "Can this be Naomi?"

"Don't call me Naomi," she told them. "Call me Mara, because the Almighty has made my life very bitter. I went away full, but the LORD has brought me back empty. Why call me Naomi? The LORD has afflicted me; the Almighty has brought misfortune upon me."

So Naomi returned from Moab accompanied by Ruth the Moabitess, her daughter-in-law, arriving in Bethlehem as the barley harvest was beginning...

Now Naomi had a relative on her husband's side, from the clan of Elimelech, a man of standing, whose name was Boaz...

Boaz replied, "I've been told all about what you have done for your mother-in-law since the death of your husband—how you left your father and mother and your homeland and came to live with a people you did not know before.

"The LORD bless him!" Naomi said to her daughter-in-law. "He has not stopped showing his kindness to the living and the dead." She added, "That man is our close relative; he is one of our kinsman-redeemers."

One day Naomi her mother-in-law said to her, "My daughter, should I not try to find a home for you, where you will be well provided for?

Stay here for the night, and in the morning if he wants to redeem, good; let him redeem. But if he is not willing, as surely as the LORD lives I will do it. Lie here until morning." ... When Ruth came to her mother-in-law, Naomi asked, "How did it go, my daughter?" ... Then she told her everything Boaz had done for her and added, "He gave me these six measures of barley, saying, 'Don't go back to your mother-in-law empty-handed.'"

Orpah

Ruth 1:1-14 AMP

In the days when the judges ruled, there was a famine in the land. And a certain man of Bethlehem of Judah went to sojourn in the country of Moab, he, his wife, and his two sons.

The man's name was Elimelech and his wife's name was Naomi and his two sons were named Mahlon [invalid] and Chilion [pining]; they were Ephrathites from Bethlehem of Judah. They went to the country of Moab and continued there.

But Elimelech, who Naomi's husband, died, and she was left with her two sons.

And they took wives of the women of Moab; the name of the one was Orpah and the name of the other Ruth. They dwelt there about ten years;

And Mahlon and Chilion died also, both of them, so the woman was bereft of her two sons and her husband.

Then she arose with her daughters-in-law to return from the country of Moab, for she had heard in Moab how the Lord had visited His people in giving them food.

So she left the place where she was, her two daughters-in-law with her, and they started on the way back to Judah.

But Naomi said to her two daughters-in-law, Go, return each of you to her mother's house. May the Lord deal kindly with you, as you have dealt with the dead and with me.

The Lord grant that you may find a home and rest, each in the house of her husband! Then she kissed them and they wept aloud.

And they said to her, No, we will return with you to your people.

But Naomi said, Turn back, my daughters, why will you go with me? Have I yet sons in my womb that may become your husbands?

Turn back, my daughters, go; for I am too old to have a husband. If I should say I have hope, even if I should have a husband tonight and should bear sons,

Would you therefore wait till they were grown? Would you therefore refrain from marrying? No, my daughters; it is far more bitter for me than for you that the hand of the Lord is gone out against me.

Then they wept aloud again; and Orpah kissed her mother-in-law [good-bye], but Ruth clung to her.

Pharaoh's Daughter

Exodus 2:5-10 NLT

... one of Pharaoh's daughters came down to bathe in the river, and her servant girls walked along the riverbank. When the princess saw the little basket among the reeds, she told one of her servant girls to get it for her. As the princess opened it, she found the baby boy. His helpless cries touched her heart. "He must be one of the Hebrew children," she said.

Then the baby's sister approached the princess. "Should I go and find one of the Hebrew women to nurse the baby for you?" she asked.

"Yes, do!" the princess replied. So the girl rushed home and called the baby's mother.

"Take this child home and nurse him for me," the princess told her. "I will pay you for your help." So the baby's mother took her baby home and nursed him.

Later, when he was older, the child's mother brought him back to the princess, who adopted him as her son. The princess named him Moses, for she said, "I drew him out of the water."

Acts 7:20-22 NIV

"At that time Moses was born, and he was no ordinary child. For three months he was cared for in his father's house. When he was placed outside, Pharaoh's daughter took him and brought him up as her own son. Moses was educated in all the wisdom of the Egyptians and was powerful in speech and action.

Hebrews 11:24-25 KJV

By faith Moses, when he was come to years, refused to be called the son of Pharaoh's daughter; Choosing rather to suffer affliction with the people of God, than to enjoy the pleasures of sin for a season.

Potiphar's Wife

Genesis 39:1-2, 6-21 NLT

Now when Joseph arrived in Egypt with the Ishmaelite traders, he was purchased by Potiphar, a member of the personal staff of Pharaoh, the king of Egypt. Potiphar was the captain of the palace guard.

The LORD was with Joseph and blessed him greatly as he served in the home of his Egyptian master ... Now Joseph was a very handsome and well-built young man. And about this time, Potiphar's wife began to desire him and invited him to sleep with her. But Joseph refused. "Look," he told her, "my master trusts me with everything in his entire household. No one here has more authority than I do! He has held back nothing from me except you, because you are his wife. How could I ever do such a wicked thing? It would be a great sin against God."

She kept putting pressure on him day after day, but he refused to sleep with her, and he kept out of her way as much as possible. One day, however, no one else was around when he was doing his work inside the house. She came and grabbed him by his shirt, demanding, "Sleep with me!" Joseph tore himself away, but as he did, his shirt came off. She was left holding it as he ran from the house.

When she saw that she had his shirt and that he had fled, she began screaming. Soon all the men around the place came running. "My husband has brought this Hebrew slave here to insult us!" she sobbed. "He tried to rape me, but I screamed. When he heard my loud cries, he ran and left his shirt behind with me."

She kept the shirt with her, and when her husband came home that night, she told him her story. "That Hebrew slave you've had around here tried to make a fool of me," she said. "I was saved only by my screams. He ran out, leaving his shirt behind!"

After hearing his wife's story, Potiphar was furious! He took Joseph and threw him into the prison where the king's prisoners were held. But the LORD was with Joseph there, too, and he granted Joseph favor with the chief jailer ...

Queen of Sheba

1 Kings 10:1-13 KJV

And when the queen of Sheba heard of the fame of Solomon concerning the name of the LORD, she came to prove him with hard questions.

And she came to Jerusalem with a very great train, with camels that bare spices, and very much gold, and precious stones:and when she was come to Solomon, she communed with him of all that was in her heart. And Solomon told her all her questions:there was not any thing hid from the king, which he told her not.

And when the queen of Sheba had seen all Solomon's wisdom, and the house that he had built,

And the meat of his table, and the sitting of his servants, and the attendance of his ministers, and their apparel, and his cupbearers, and his ascent by which he went up unto the house of the LORD; there was no more spirit in her.

And she said to the king, It was a true report that I heard in mine own land of thy acts and of thy wisdom.

Howbeit I believed not the words, until I came, and mine eyes had seen it: nd, behold, the half was not told me: thy wisdom and prosperity exceedeth the fame which I heard.

Happy are thy men, happy are these thy servants, which stand continually before thee, and that hear thy wisdom.

Blessed be the LORD thy God, which delighted in thee, to set thee on the throne of Israel: because the LORD loved Israel for ever, therefore made he thee king, to do judgment and justice.

And she gave the king an hundred and twenty talents of gold, and of spices very great store, and precious stones:there came no more such abundance of spices as these ...

And the navy also of Hiram, that brought gold from Ophir, brought in from Ophir great plenty of almug trees, and precious stones. And the king made of the almug trees pillars for the house of the LORD, and for the king's house, harps also and psalteries for singers:there came no such almug trees, nor were seen unto this day.

And king Solomon gave unto the queen of Sheba all her desire, whatsoever she asked, beside that which Solomon gave her of his royal bounty. So she turned and went to her own country, she and her servants.

Rachel

Genesis 29:16-18, 20, 25-28, 31:30:1-2, 5-8, 22, 24; 31:2-3, 19, 24-26, 33-35; 35:17-19 KJV

Laban had two daughters:... the elder *was* Leah ... the younger *was* Rachel ... Rachel was beautiful and well favoured. Jacob loved Rachel ... served seven years for Rachel ... seemed unto him *but* a few days, for the love he had to her.

... in the morning, behold, it *was* Leah: and he said to Laban, What *is* this thou hast done unto me? did not I serve with thee for Rachel ... thou beguiled me? And Laban said, It must not be so done in our country, to give the younger before the firstborn. ... serve with me yet seven other years ... and he gave him Rachel his daughter to wife also.

And when the LORD saw that Leah *was* hated, he opened her womb: but Rachel *was* barren ... Rachel envied her sister; and said unto Jacob, Give me children, or else I die ...

And Bilhah [Rachel's handmaid] conceived and bare Jacob a son ... Dan ... became pregnant again ... a second son. Rachel named him Naphtali, for she said, "I have had an intense struggle with my sister, and I am winning!"

Then God remembered Rachel's plight and answered her prayers by giving her a child. And she named him Joseph, for she said, "May the LORD give me yet another son."

And Jacob began to notice a considerable cooling in Laban's attitude toward him. Then the LORD said to Jacob, "Return to the land of your father and grandfather and to your relatives there, and I will be with you."

At the time they left, Laban was some distance away, shearing his sheep. Rachel stole her father's household gods and took them with her.

But the previous night God had appeared to Laban in a dream. "Be careful about what you say to Jacob!" he was told.

So when Laban caught up with Jacob as he was camped in the hill country of Gilead ... "What do you mean by sneaking off like this ... Are my daughters prisoners, the plunder of war, that you have stolen them away like this?

Laban went first into Jacob's tent to search there, then into Leah's ... then ... the two concubines, but he didn't find the gods. Finally, he went into Rachel's tent. Rachel had taken the household gods and had stuffed them into her camel saddle, and now she was sitting on them. ... he couldn't find them. "Forgive my not getting up, Father," Rachel explained. "I'm having my monthly period." So despite his thorough search, Laban didn't find them.

And it came to pass, when she was in hard labour, that the midwife said unto her, Fear not; thou shalt have this son also. And it came to pass, as her soul was in departing, (for she died) that she called his name Benoni: but his father called him Benjamin. And Rachel died, and was buried in the way to Ephrath, which *is* Bethlehem.

Rahab

Joshua 2:1-21 NIV

Then Joshua son of Nun secretly sent two spies from Shittim. "Go, look over the land," he said, "especially Jericho." So they went and entered the house of a prostitute named Rahab and stayed there ... So the king of Jericho sent this message to Rahab: "Bring out the men ...But the woman had taken the two men and hidden them ...

Before the spies lay down for the night, she went up on the roof and said to them, "I know that the LORD has given this land to you and that a great fear of you has fallen on us, so that all who live in this country are melting in fear because of you. We have heard how the LORD dried up the water of the Red Sea for you when you came out of Egypt, and what you did to Sihon and Og, the two kings of the Amorites east of the Jordan, whom you completely destroyed. When we heard of it, our hearts melted and everyone's courage failed because of you, for the LORD your God is God in heaven above and on the earth below ... Give me a sure sign that you will spare the lives of my father and mother, my brothers and sisters, and all who belong to them, and that you will save us from death ..."

So she let them down by a rope through the window, for the house she lived in was part of the city wall. Now she had said to them, "Go to the hills so the pursuers will not find you. Hide yourselves there three days until they return, and then go on your way." The men said to her, "This oath you made us swear will not be binding on us unless, when we enter the land, you have tied this scarlet cord in the window through which you let us down, and unless you have brought your father and mother, your brothers and all your family into your house. "Agreed," she replied. "Let it be as you say." So she sent them away and they departed. And she tied the scarlet cord in the window.

Joshua 6:27 KJV

And Joshua saved Rahab the harlot alive, and her father's household, and all that she had; and she dwelleth in Israel even unto this day; because she hid the messengers, which Joshua sent to spy out Jericho.

Hebrews 11:31 NLT

It was by faith that Rahab the prostitute did not die with all the others in her city who refused to obey God. For she had given a friendly welcome to the spies.

Rebekak

Genesis 24:2-4 NLT

One day Abraham said to the man in charge of his household, who was his oldest servant, "...Go instead to my homeland, to my relatives, and find a wife there for my son Isaac."

Genesis 24:15-17, 34-37, 58-59, 64, 67 NIV

Before he had finished praying, Rebekah came out with her jar on her shoulder. She was the daughter of Bethuel son of Milcah, who was the wife of Abraham's brother Nahor. The girl was very beautiful, a virgin; no man had ever lain with her. She went down to the spring, filled her jar and came up again.

So he said, "I am Abraham's servant. The LORD has blessed my master abundantly, and he has become wealthy. He has given him sheep and cattle, silver and gold, menservants and maidservants, and camels and donkeys. My master's wife Sarah has borne him a son in her old age, and he has given him everything he owns. And my master made me swear an oath, and said, 'You must not get a wife for my son from the daughters of the Canaanites, in whose land I live,

So they called Rebekah and asked her, "Will you go with this man?"

"I will go," she said.

So they sent their sister Rebekah on her way, along with her nurse and Abraham's servant and his men.

Rebekah also looked up and saw Isaac. She got down from her camel Isaac brought her into the tent of his mother Sarah, and he married Rebekah. So she became his wife, and he loved her; and Isaac was comforted after his mother's death.

Genesis 25:20-28 KJV

And Isaac was forty years old when he took Rebekah to wife, the daughter of Bethuel the Syrian of

Padanaram, the sister to Laban the Syrian. And Isaac entreated the LORD for his wife, because she *was* barren:and the LORD was entreated of him, and Rebekah his wife conceived. And the children struggled together within her; and she said, If *it be* so, why *am* I thus?

And she went to inquire of the LORD. And the LORD said unto her, Two nations *are* in thy womb, and two manner of people shall be separated from thy bowels; and *the one* people shall be stronger than *the other* people; and the elder shall serve the younger. And when her days to be delivered were fulfilled, behold, *there were* twins in her womb. And the first came out red, all over like an hairy garment; and they called his name Esau. And after that came his brother out, and his hand took hold on Esau's heel; and his name was called Jacob:and Isaac *was* threescore years old when she bare them. And the boys grew:and Esau was a cunning hunter, a man of the field; and Jacob *was* a plain man, dwelling in tents. And Isaac loved Esau, because he did eat of *his* venison:but Rebekah loved Jacob.

Rizpah

2 Samuel 3-8a NLT

One day Ishbosheth, Saul's son, accused Abner of sleeping with one of his father's concubines, a woman named Rizpah. Abner became furious.

2 Samuel 21:8-14 NLT

But he gave them Saul's two sons Armoni and Mephibosheth, whose mother was Rizpah daughter of Aiah. He also gave them the five sons of Saul's daughter Merab, the wife of Adriel son of Barzillai from Meholah. The men of Gibeon executed them on the mountain before the LORD. So all seven of them died together at the beginning of the barley harvest.

Then Rizpah, the mother of two of the men, spread sackcloth on a rock and stayed there the entire harvest season. She prevented vultures from tearing at their bodies during the day and stopped wild animals from eating them at night. When David learned what Rizpah, Saul's concubine, had done, he went to the people of Jabesh-gilead and asked for the bones of Saul and his son Jonathan. (When Saul and Jonathan had died in a battle with the Philistines, it was the people of Jabesh-gilead who had retrieved their bodies from the public square of the Philistine city of Beth-shan.) So David brought the bones of Saul and Jonathan, as well as the bones of the men the Gibeonites had executed. He buried them all in the tomb of Kish, Saul's father, at the town of Zela in the land of Benjamin. After that, God ended the famine in the land of Israel.

Ruth

Ruth 1:3-5, 14, 19; 2:1, 11; 3:1, 6-12; 4:1, 9-13, 17 KJV

And Elimelech Naomi's husband died; and she was left, and her two sons. And they took them wives of the women of Moab ... Orpah, and ... Ruth:and they dwelled there about ten years. And Mahlon and Chilion died also both of them; and the woman was left of her two sons and her husband.

... Orpah kissed her mother in law [goodbye]; but Ruth clave unto her.

So they two went until they came to Bethlehem ... all the city was moved about them ... Naomi had a kinsman of her husband's, a mighty man of wealth, of the family of Elimelech; and his name *was* Boaz.

And Boaz answered and said unto her [Ruth], It hath fully been showed me, all that thou hast done unto thy mother in law since the death of thine husband: and *how* thou hast left thy father and thy mother, and the land of thy nativity, and art come unto a people which thou knewest not heretofore.

... his heart was merry, he went to lie down at the end of the heap of corn: and she came softly, and uncovered his feet, and laid her down. And it came to pass at midnight, that the man was afraid, and turned himself: and, behold, a woman lay at his feet. And he said, Who *art* thou? And she answered, I *am* Ruth thine handmaid: spread therefore thy skirt over thine handmaid; for thou *art* a near kinsman. And he said, Blessed *be* thou of the LORD, my daughter: *for* thou hast showed more kindness in the latter end than at the beginning, inasmuch as thou followedst not young men, whether poor or rich. And now, my daughter, fear not; I will do to thee all that thou requirest:for all the city of my people doth know that thou *art* a virtuous woman. And now it is true that I *am thy* near kinsman:howbeit there is a kinsman nearer than I.

And Boaz said unto the elders, and *unto* all the people, Ye *are* witnesses this day, that I have bought all that *was* Elimelech's, and all that *was* Chilion's and Mahlon's, of the hand of Naomi. Moreover Ruth the Moabitess, the wife of Mahlon, have I purchased to be my wife, to raise up the name of the dead upon his inheritance, that the name of the dead be not cut off from among his brethren, and from the gate of his place:ye *are* witnesses this day. And all the people that *were* in the gate, and the elders, said, *We are* witnesses. The LORD make the woman that is come into thine house like Rachel and like Leah, which two did build the house of Israel:and do thou worthily in Ephratah, and be famous in Bethlehem:And let thy house be like the house of Pharez, whom Tamar bare unto Judah, of the seed which the LORD shall give thee of this young woman.

So Boaz took Ruth, and she was his wife:and when he went in unto her, the LORD gave her conception, and she bare a son.

And the women her neighbours gave it a name, saying, There is a son born to Naomi; and they called his name Obed:he *is* the father of Jesse, the father of David.

Samson's Mother

Judges 13:2-6, 9-13, 19-20, 24 NIV)

A certain man of Zorah, named Manoah, from the clan of the Danites, had a wife who was sterile and remained childless. The angel of the LORD appeared to her and said, "You are sterile and childless, but you are going to conceive and have a son. Now see to it that you drink no wine or other fermented drink and that you do not eat anything unclean, because you will conceive and give birth to a son. No razor may be used on his head, because the boy is to be a Nazirite, set apart to God from birth, and he will begin the deliverance of Israel from the hands of the Philistines."

Then the woman went to her husband and told him, "A man of God came to me. He looked like an angel of God, very awesome. I didn't ask him where he came from, and he didn't tell me his name.

God heard Manoah, and the angel of God came again to the woman while she was out in the field; but her husband Manoah was not with her. The woman hurried to tell her husband, "He's here! The man who appeared to me the other day!"

Manoah got up and followed his wife. When he came to the man, he said, "Are you the one who talked to my wife?"

"I am," he said.

So Manoah asked him, "When your words are fulfilled, what is to be the rule for the boy's life and work?"

The angel of the LORD answered, "Your wife must do all that I have told her.

Then Manoah took a young goat, together with the grain offering, and sacrificed it on a rock to the LORD . And the LORD did an amazing thing while Manoah and his wife watched:As the flame blazed up from the altar toward heaven, the angel of the LORD ascended in the flame. Seeing this, Manoah and his wife fell with their faces to the ground.

The woman gave birth to a boy and named him Samson. He grew and the LORD blessed him ...

Sarah

Genesis 17:15-16; 19-21 KJV

And God said unto Abraham, As for Sarai thy wife, thou shalt not call her name Sarai, but Sarah shall her name be. And I will bless her, and give thee a son also of her:yea, I will bless her, and she shall be a *mother* of nations; kings of people shall be of her.

And God said, Sarah thy wife shall bear thee a son indeed; and thou shalt call his name Isaac:and I will establish my covenant with him for an everlasting covenant, *and* with his seed after him. And as for Ishmael, I have heard thee:Behold, I have blessed him, and will make him fruitful, and will multiply him exceedingly; twelve princes shall he beget, and I will make him a great nation. But my covenant will I establish with Isaac, which Sarah shall bear unto thee at this set time in the next year.

Genesis 18:6-12; 21:1,4-5; 23:1 NIV

"Where is your wife Sarah?" they asked him.

"There, in the tent," he said.

Then the LORD said, "I will surely return to you about this time next year, and Sarah your wife will have a son."

Now Sarah was listening at the entrance to the tent, which was behind him. Abraham and Sarah were already old and well advanced in years, and Sarah was past the age of childbearing. So Sarah laughed to herself as she thought, "After I am worn out and my master is old, will I now have this pleasure?"

And the LORD visited Sarah as he had said, and the LORD did unto Sarah as he had spoken. And Abraham circumcised his son Isaac being eight days old, as God had commanded him. And Abraham was an hundred years old, when his son Isaac was born unto him.

Sarah lived to be a hundred and twenty-seven years old. She died at Kiriath Arba (that is, Hebron) in the land of Canaan, and Abraham went to mourn for Sarah and to weep over her.

Solomon's Wives

1 Kings 11:1-8 NLT

Now King Solomon loved many foreign women. Besides Pharaoh's daughter, he married women from Moab, Ammon, Edom, Sidon, and from among the Hittites. The LORD had clearly instructed his people not to intermarry with those nations, because the women they married would lead them to worship their gods. Yet Solomon insisted on loving them anyway.

He had seven hundred wives and three hundred concubines. And sure enough, they led his heart away from the LORD. In Solomon's old age, they turned his heart to worship their gods instead of trusting only in the LORD his God, as his father, David, had done. Solomon worshiped Ashtoreth, the goddess of the Sidonians, and Molech, the detestable god of the Ammonites.

Thus, Solomon did what was evil in the LORD'S sight; he refused to follow the LORD completely, as his father, David, had done. On the Mount of Olives, east of Jerusalem, he even built a shrine for Chemosh, the detestable god of Moab, and another for Molech, the detestable god of the Ammonites. Solomon built such shrines for all his foreign wives to use for burning incense and sacrificing to their gods.

Tamar

1 Samuel 13:1-5, 8-16, 28-29, 37-39 NLT

David's son Absalom had a beautiful sister named Tamar. And Amnon, her half brother, fell desperately in love with her. Amnon became so obsessed with Tamar that he became ill. She was a virgin, and it seemed impossible that he could ever fulfill his love for her.

Now Amnon had a very crafty friend—his cousin Jonadab. He was the son of David's brother Shimea. One day Jonadab said to Amnon, "What's the trouble? Why should the son of a king look so dejected morning after morning?"

So Amnon told him, "I am in love with Tamar, Absalom's sister."

"Well," Jonadab said, "I'll tell you what to do. Go back to bed and pretend you are sick. When your father comes to see you, ask him to let Tamar come and prepare some food for you. Tell him you'll feel better if she feeds you."

When Tamar arrived at Amnon's house, she went to the room where he was lying down so he could watch her mix some dough. Then she baked some special bread for him. But when she set the serving tray before him, he refused to eat. "Everyone get out of here," Amnon told his servants. So they all left. Then he said to Tamar, "Now bring the food into my bedroom and feed it to me here." So Tamar took it to him. But as she was feeding him, he grabbed her and demanded, "Come to bed with me, my darling sister."

"No, my brother!" she cried. "Don't be foolish! Don't do this to me! You know what a serious crime it is to do such a thing in Israel. Where could I go in my shame? And you would be called one of the greatest fools in Israel. Please, just speak to the king about it, and he will let you marry me."

But Amnon wouldn't listen to her, and since he was stronger than she was, he raped her. Suddenly Amnon's love turned to hate, and he hated her even more than he had loved her. "Get out of here!" he snarled at her.

"No, no!" Tamar cried. "To reject me now is a greater wrong than what you have already done to me."

Absalom told his men, "Wait until Amnon gets drunk; then at my signal, kill him! Don't be afraid. I'm the one who has given the command. Take courage and do it!" So at Absalom's signal they murdered Amnon. Then the other sons of the king jumped on their mules and fled.

Absalom fled to his grandfather, Talmai son of Ammihud, the king of Geshur. He stayed there in Geshur for three years. And David, now reconciled to Amnon's death, longed to be reunited with his son Absalom.

Two Harlot Mothers (with Solomon)

1 Kings 3:16-28 NIV

Now two prostitutes [harlots - KJV] came to the king and stood before him. One of them said, "My lord, this woman and I live in the same house. I had a baby while she was there with me. The third day after my child was born, this woman also had a baby. We were alone; there was no one in the house but the two of us.

"During the night this woman's son died because she lay on him. So she got up in the middle of the night and took my son from my side while I your servant was asleep. She put him by her breast and put her dead son by my breast. The next morning, I got up to nurse my son-and he was dead! But when I looked at him closely in the morning light, I saw that it wasn't the son I had borne."

The other woman said, "No! The living one is my son; the dead one is yours."

But the first one insisted, "No! The dead one is yours; the living one is mine." And so they argued before the king.

The king said, "This one says, 'My son is alive and your son is dead,' while that one says, 'No! Your son is dead and mine is alive.' "

Then the king said, "Bring me a sword." So they brought a sword for the king. He then gave an order:"Cut the living child in two and give half to one and half to the other."

The woman whose son was alive was filled with compassion for her son and said to the king, "Please, my lord, give her the living baby! Don't kill him!"

But the other said, "Neither I nor you shall have him. Cut him in two!"

Then the king gave his ruling:"Give the living baby to the first woman. Do not kill him; she is his mother."

When all Israel heard the verdict the king had given, they held the king in awe, because they saw that he had wisdom from God to administer justice.

Vashti

Esther 1:1, 3-5, 7-12, 17-19; 2:1-2, 4, 7 KJV

Now it came to pass in the days of Ahasuerus, (this *is* Ahasuerus which reigned, from India even unto Ethiopia, *over* an hundred and seven and twenty provinces:) … In the third year of his reign, he made a feast unto all his princes and his servants; the power of Persia and Media, the nobles and princes of the provinces, *being* before him:When he showed the riches of his glorious kingdom and the honour of his excellent majesty many days, *even* an hundred and fourscore days. And when these days were expired, the king made a feast unto all the people that were present in Shushan the palace, both unto great and small, seven days, in the court of the garden of the king's palace;

And they gave *them* drink in vessels of gold, (the vessels being diverse one from another,) and royal wine in abundance, according to the state of the king. And the drinking *was* according to the law; none did compel:for so the king had appointed to all the officers of his house, that they should do according to every man's pleasure. Also Vashti the queen made a feast for the women *in* the royal house which *belonged* to king Ahasuerus.

On the seventh day, when the heart of the king was merry with wine, he commanded Mehuman, Biztha, Harbona, Bigtha, and Abagtha, Zethar, and Carcas, the seven chamberlains that served in the presence of Ahasuerus the king, To bring Vashti the queen before the king with the crown royal, to show the people and the princes her beauty:for she *was* fair to look on.

For *this* deed of the queen shall come abroad unto all women, so that they shall despise their husbands in their eyes, when it shall be reported, The king Ahasuerus commanded Vashti the queen to be brought in before him, but she came not. *Likewise* shall the ladies of Persia and Media say this day unto all the king's princes, which have heard of the deed of the queen. Thus *shall there arise* too much contempt and wrath. If it please the king, let there go a royal commandment from him, and let it be written among the laws of the Persians and the Medes, that it be not altered, That Vashti come no more before king Ahasuerus; and let the king give her royal estate unto another that is better than she.

After these things, when the wrath of king Ahasuerus was appeased, he remembered Vashti, and what she had done, and what was decreed against her. Then said the king's servants that ministered unto him, Let there be fair young virgins sought for the king:And let the maiden which pleaseth the king be queen instead of Vashti. And the thing pleased the king; and he did so.

And he brought up Hadassah, that *is*, Esther, his uncle's daughter:for she had neither father nor mother, and the maid *was* fair and beautiful; whom Mordecai, when her father and mother were dead, took for his own daughter.

Widow at Zarephath

I Kings 17:8-24 KJV

And the word of the LORD came unto him, saying, Arise, get thee to Zarephath, which belongeth to Zidon, and dwell there:behold, I have commanded a widow woman there to sustain thee.

So he arose and went to Zarephath. And when he came to the gate of the city, behold, the widow woman was there gathering of sticks:and he called to her, and said, Fetch me, I pray thee, a little water in a vessel, that I may drink. And as she was going to fetch it, he called to her, and said, Bring me, I pray thee, a morsel of bread in thine hand.

And she said, As the LORD thy God liveth, I have not a cake, but an handful of meal in a barrel, and a little oil in a cruse:and, behold, I am gathering two sticks, that I may go in and dress it for me and my son, that we may eat it, and die. And Elijah said unto her, Fear not; go and do as thou hast said:but make me thereof a little cake first, and bring it unto me, and after make for thee and for thy son.

For thus saith the LORD God of Israel, The barrel of meal shall not waste, neither shall the cruse of oil fail, until the day that the LORD sendeth rain upon the earth.

And she went and did according to the saying of Elijah:and she, and he, and her house, did eat many days ... And it came to pass after these things, that the son of the woman, the mistress of the house, fell sick; and his sickness was so sore, that there was no breath left in him.

And she said unto Elijah, What have I to do with thee, O thou man of God? art thou come unto me to call my sin to remembrance, and to slay my son? And he said unto her, Give me thy son. And he took him out of her bosom, and carried him up into a loft, where he abode, and laid him upon his own bed.

And he cried unto the LORD, and said, O LORD my God, hast thou also brought evil upon the widow with whom I sojourn, by slaying her son?

And he stretched himself upon the child three times, and cried unto the LORD, and said, O LORD my God, I pray thee, let this child's soul come into him again.

And the LORD heard the voice of Elijah; and the soul of the child came into him again, and he revived. And Elijah took the child, and brought him down out of the chamber into the house, and delivered him unto his mother:and Elijah said, See, thy son liveth.

And the woman said to Elijah, Now by this I know that thou art a man of God, and that the word of the LORD in thy mouth is truth.

Widow's Oil

2 Kings 4:1-7 NIV

The wife of a man from the company of the prophets cried out to Elisha, "Your servant my husband is dead, and you know that he revered the LORD. But now his creditor is coming to take my two boys as his slaves."

Elisha replied to her, "How can I help you? Tell me, what do you have in your house?"

"Your servant has nothing there at all," she said, "except a little oil."

Elisha said, "Go around and ask all your neighbors for empty jars. Don't ask for just a few. Then go inside and shut the door behind you and your sons. Pour oil into all the jars, and as each is filled, put it to one side."

She left him and afterward shut the door behind her and her sons. They brought the jars to her and she kept pouring. When all the jars were full, she said to her son, "Bring me another one."

But he replied, "There is not a jar left." Then the oil stopped flowing.

She went and told the man of God, and he said, "Go, sell the oil and pay your debts. You and your sons can live on what is left."

Wise Woman of Abel

2 Samuel 20:16-22 KJV

Then cried a wise woman out of the city, Hear, hear; say, I pray you, unto Joab, Come near hither, that I may speak with thee. And when he was come near unto her, the woman said, *Art* thou Joab? And he answered, I *am he*. Then she said unto him, Hear the words of thine handmaid. And he answered, I do hear. Then she spake, saying, They were wont to speak in old time, saying, They shall surely ask *counsel* at Abel: and so they ended *the matter. I am one of them that are* peaceable *and* faithful in Israel: thou seekest to destroy a city and a mother in Israel: why wilt thou swallow up the inheritance of the LORD? And Joab answered and said, Far be it, far be it from me, that I should swallow up or destroy. The matter *is* not so: but a man of mount Ephraim, Sheba the son of Bichri by name, hath lifted up his hand against the king, *even* against David: deliver him only, and I will depart from the city. And the woman said unto Joab, Behold, his head shall be thrown to thee over the wall. Then the woman went unto all the people in her wisdom. And they cut off the head of Sheba the son of Bichri, and cast *it* out to Joab. And he blew a trumpet, and they retired from the city, every man to his tent. And Joab returned to Jerusalem unto the king.

Wide Woman of Tekoah

11 Samuel 14:1-20 NLT

Joab realized how much the king longed to see Absalom. So he sent for a woman from Tekoa who had a reputation for great wisdom. He said to her, "Pretend you are in mourning; wear mourning clothes and don't put on lotions. Act like a woman who has been mourning for the dead for a long time. Then go to the king and tell him the story I am about to tell you." Then Joab told her what to say.

When the woman from Tekoa approached the king, she bowed with her face to the ground in deep respect and cried out, "O king! Help me!"

"What's the trouble?" the king asked.

"Alas, I am a widow!" she replied. "My husband is dead. My two sons had a fight out in the field. And since no one was there to stop it, one of them was killed. Now the rest of the family is demanding, 'Let us have your son. We will execute him for murdering his brother. He doesn't deserve to inherit his family's property.' They want to extinguish the only coal I have left, and my husband's name and family will disappear from the face of the earth."

"Leave it to me," the king told her. "Go home, and I'll see to it that no one touches him."

"Oh, thank you, my lord the king," the woman from Tekoa replied. "If you are criticized for helping me, let the blame fall on me and on my father's house, and let the king and his throne be innocent."

"If anyone objects," the king said, "bring him to me. I can assure you he will never complain again!"

Then she said, "Please swear to me by the Lord your God that you won't let anyone take vengeance against my son. I want no more bloodshed."

"As surely as the Lord lives," he replied, "not a hair on your son's head will be disturbed!"

"Please allow me to ask one more thing of my lord the king," she said.

"Go ahead and speak," he responded.

She replied, "Why don't you do as much for the people of God as you have promised to do for me? You have convicted yourself in making this decision, because you have refused to bring home your own banished son. All of us must die eventually. Our lives are like water spilled out on the ground, which cannot be gathered up again. But God does not just sweep life away; instead, he devises ways to bring us back when we have been separated from him.

"I have come to plead with my lord the king because people have threatened me. I said to myself, 'Perhaps the king will listen to me and rescue us from those who would cut us off from the inheritance God has given us. Yes, my lord the king will give us peace of mind again.' I know that you are like an angel of God in discerning good from evil. May the Lord your God be with you."

"I must know one thing," the king replied, "and tell me the truth."

"Yes, my lord the king," she responded.

"Did Joab put you up to this?"

And the woman replied, "My lord the king, how can I deny it? Nobody can hide anything from you. Yes, Joab sent me and told me what to say. He did it to place the matter before you in a different light. But you are as wise as an angel of God, and you understand everything that happens among us!"

Wisehearted Women

Exodus 35:22-29 KJVs

And they came, both men and women, as many as were willing hearted, and brought bracelets, and earrings, and rings, and tablets, all jewels of gold: and every man that offered offered an offering of gold unto the LORD.

And every man, with whom was found blue, and purple, and scarlet, and fine linen, and goats' hair, and red skins of rams, and badgers' skins, brought them.

Every one that did offer an offering of silver and brass brought the Lord's offering: and every man, with whom was found shittim wood for any work of the service, brought it.

And all the women that were wise hearted did spin with their hands, and brought that which they had spun, both of blue, and of purple, and of scarlet, and of fine linen.

And all the women whose heart stirred them up in wisdom spun goats' hair.

And the rulers brought onyx stones, and stones to be set, for the ephod, and for the breastplate;

And spice, and oil for the light, and for the anointing oil, and for the sweet incense.

The children of Israel brought a willing offering unto the Lord, every man and woman, whose heart made them willing to bring for all manner of work, which the Lord had commanded to be made by the hand of Moses.

Woman of Thebez

Judges 9:50-57 NIV

Next Abimelech went to Thebez and besieged it and captured it. Inside the city, however, was a strong tower, to which all the men and women-all the people of the city-fled. They locked themselves in and climbed up on the tower roof. Abimelech went to the tower and stormed it. But as he approached the entrance to the tower to set it on fire, a woman dropped an upper millstone on his head and cracked his skull.

Hurriedly he called to his armor-bearer, "Draw your sword and kill me, so that they can't say, 'A woman killed him.' "So his servant ran him through, and he died. When the Israelites saw that Abimelech was dead, they went home.

Thus God repaid the wickedness that Abimelech had done to his father by murdering his seventy brothers. God also made the men of Shechem pay for all their wickedness. The curse of Jotham son of Jerub-Baal came on them.

Woman with Familiar Spirit at Endor

1 Samuel 28:3, 5-11, 16-25 NIV

Now Samuel was dead, and all Israel had mourned for him and buried him in his own town of Ramah. Saul had expelled the mediums and spiritists from the land ...

When Saul saw the Philistine army, he was afraid; terror filled his heart. He inquired of the LORD, but the LORD did not answer him by dreams or Urim or prophets. Saul then said to his attendants, "Find me a woman who is a medium, so I may go and inquire of her."

"There is one in Endor," they said.

So Saul disguised himself, putting on other clothes, and at night he and two men went to the woman. "Consult a spirit for me," he said, "and bring up for me the one I name."

But the woman said to him, "Surely you know what Saul has done. He has cut off the mediums and spiritists from the land. Why have you set a trap for my life to bring about my death?"

Saul swore to her by the LORD, "As surely as the LORD lives, you will not be punished for this."

Then the woman asked, "Whom shall I bring up for you?"

"Bring up Samuel," he said.

Samuel said, "Why do you consult me, now that the LORD has turned away from you and become your enemy? The LORD has done what he predicted through me. The LORD has torn the kingdom out of your hands and given it to one of your neighbors-to David. Because you did not obey the LORD or carry out his fierce wrath against the Amalekites, the LORD has done this to you today. The LORD will hand over both Israel and you to the Philistines, and tomorrow you and your sons will be with me. The LORD will also hand over the army of Israel to the Philistines."

Immediately Saul fell full length on the ground, filled with fear because of Samuel's words. His strength was gone, for he had eaten nothing all that day and night.

When the woman came to Saul and saw that he was greatly shaken, she said, "Look, your maidservant has obeyed you. I took my life in my hands and did what you told me to do. Now please listen to your servant and let me give you some food so you may eat and have the strength to go on your way."

He refused and said, "I will not eat." But his men joined the woman in urging him ... He got up from the ground and sat on the couch.

The woman had a fattened calf at the house, which she butchered at once. She took some flour, kneaded it and baked bread without yeast. Then she set it before Saul and his men, and they ate. That same night they got up and left.

Zipporah (Moses' Wife)

Exodus 2:16-22 NIV

Now a priest of Midian had seven daughters, and they came to draw water and fill the troughs to water their father's flock. Some shepherds came along and drove them away, but Moses got up and came to their rescue and watered their flock.

When the girls returned to Reuel their father, he asked them, "Why have you returned so early today?"

They answered, "An Egyptian rescued us from the shepherds. He even drew water for us and watered the flock."

"And where is he?" he asked his daughters. "Why did you leave him? Invite him to have something to eat."

Moses agreed to stay with the man, who gave his daughter Zipporah to Moses in marriage. Zipporah gave birth to a son, and Moses named him Gershom, saying, "I have become an alien in a foreign land."

Exodus 4:24-26 NIV

At a lodging place on the way, the LORD met {Moses} and was about to kill him. But Zipporah took a flint knife, cut off her son's foreskin and touched {Moses'} feet with it. "Surely you are a bridegroom of blood to me," she said. So the LORD let him alone. (At that time she said "bridegroom of blood," referring to circumcision.)

Exodus 4:1-6 NIV

Now Jethro, the priest of Midian and father-in-law of Moses, heard of everything God had done for Moses and for his people Israel, and how the LORD had brought Israel out of Egypt.

After Moses had sent away his wife Zipporah, his father-in-law Jethro received her and her two sons. One son was named Gershom, for Moses said, "I have become an alien in a foreign land"; and the other was named Eliezer, for he said, "My father's God was my helper; he saved me from the sword of Pharaoh." Jethro, Moses' father-in-law, together with Moses' sons and wife, came to him in the desert, where he was camped near the mountain of God. Jethro had sent word to him, "I, your father-in-law Jethro, am coming to you with your wife and her two sons."

.

Women in the
New Testament
of the Bible

Afflicted Daughters of Abraham

Luke 13:11-16 KJV

And, behold, there was a woman which had a spirit of infirmity eighteen years, and was bowed together, and could in no wise lift up *herself*. And when Jesus saw her, he called *her to him*, and said unto her, Woman, thou art loosed from thine infirmity. And he laid *his* hands on her: and immediately she was made straight, and glorified God. And the ruler of the synagogue answered with indignation, because that Jesus had healed on the sabbath day, and said unto the people, There are six days in which men ought to work: in them therefore come and be healed, and not on the sabbath day. The Lord then answered him, and said, *Thou* hypocrite, doth not each one of you on the sabbath loose his ox or *his* ass from the stall, and lead *him* away to watering? And ought not this woman, being a daughter of Abraham, whom Satan hath bound, lo, these eighteen years, be loosed from this bond on the sabbath day?

Anna, The Prophetess

Luke 2:36-38 KJV

And there was one Anna, a prophetess, the daughter of Phanuel, of the tribe of Aser:she was of a great age, and had lived with an husband seven years from her virginity; And she *was* a widow of about fourscore and four years, which departed not from the temple, but served *God* with fastings and prayers night and day. And she coming in that instant gave thanks likewise unto the Lord, and spake of him to all them that looked for redemption in Jerusalem.

Bernice

Acts 25:13-14, 23; 26:29-32 KJV

And after certain days king Agrippa and Bernice came unto Caesarea to salute Festus.

And when they had been there many days, Festus declared Paul's cause unto the king, saying, There is a certain man left in bonds by Felix:...

And on the morrow, when Agrippa was come, and Bernice, with great pomp, and was entered into the place of hearing, with the chief captains, and principal men of the city, at Festus' commandment Paul was brought forth...

Then Agrippa said unto Paul, Almost thou persuadest me to be a Christian.

And Paul said, I would to God, that not only thou, but also all that hear me this day, were both almost, and altogether such as I am, except these bonds.

And when he had thus spoken, the king rose up, and the governor, and Bernice, and they that sat with them:

And when they were gone aside, they talked between themselves, saying, This man doeth nothing worthy of death or of bonds.

Then said Agrippa unto Festus, This man might have been set at liberty, if he had not appealed unto Caesar.

Daughters of Jerusalem

Luke 13:11-16 KJV

And as they led him away, they laid hold upon one Simon, a Cyrenian, coming out of the country, and on him they laid the cross, that he might bear *it* after Jesus. And there followed him a great company of people, and of women, which also bewailed and lamented him. But Jesus turning unto them said, Daughters of Jerusalem, weep not for me, but weep for yourselves, and for your children. For, behold, the days are coming, in the which they shall say, Blessed *are* the barren, and the wombs that never bare, and the paps which never gave suck. Then shall they begin to say to the mountains, Fall on us; and to the hills, Cover us... (KJV)

Demon Possessed Damsel

Acts 16:16-30 KJV

And it came to pass, as we went to prayer, a certain damsel possessed with a spirit of divination met us, which brought her masters much gain by soothsaying (fortune-teller, NLT):The same followed Paul and us, and cried, saying, These men are the servants of the most high God, which show unto us the way of salvation. And this did she many days. But Paul, being grieved, turned and said to the spirit, I command thee in the name of Jesus Christ to come out of her. And he came out the same hour. And when her masters saw that the hope of their gains was gone, they caught Paul and Silas, and drew *them* into the marketplace unto the rulers, And brought them to the magistrates, saying, These men, being Jews, do exceedingly trouble our city, And teach customs, which are not lawful for us to receive, neither to observe, being Romans. And the multitude rose up together against them:and the magistrates rent off their clothes, and commanded to beat *them*. (stripped and beaten with wooden rods, NLT); And when they had laid many stripes upon them (severely flogged, NIV), they cast *them* into prison, charging the jailor to keep them safely:Who, having received such a charge, thrust them into the inner prison, and made their feet fast in the stocks.

And at midnight Paul and Silas prayed, and sang praises unto God:and the prisoners heard them. And suddenly there was a great earthquake, so that the foundations of the prison were shaken:and immediately all the doors were opened, and every one's bands were loosed. And the keeper of the prison awaking out of his sleep, and seeing the prison doors open, he drew out his sword, and would have killed himself, supposing that the prisoners had been fled. But Paul cried with a loud voice, saying, Do thyself no harm:for we are all here. Then he called for a light, and sprang in, and came trembling, and fell down before Paul and Silas, And brought them out ...

Dorcas (Tabitha)

Acts 9:36-43 NLT

There was a believer in Joppa named Tabitha (which in Greek is Dorcas). She was always doing kind things for others and helping the poor. About this time she became ill and died. Her friends prepared her for burial and laid her in an upstairs room. But they had heard that Peter was nearby at Lydda, so they sent two men to beg him, "Please come as soon as possible!"

So Peter returned with them; and as soon as he arrived, they took him to the upstairs room. The room was filled with widows who were weeping and showing him the coats and other garments Dorcas had made for them. But Peter asked them all to leave the room; then he knelt and prayed. Turning to the body he said, "Get up, Tabitha." And she opened her eyes! When she saw Peter, she sat up! He gave her his hand and helped her up. Then he called in the widows and all the believers, and he showed them that she was alive.

The news raced through the whole town, and many believed in the Lord. And Peter stayed a long time in Joppa, living with Simon, a leather-worker.

Elizabeth, Mother of John the Baptist

Luke 1 NLT

It all begins with a Jewish priest, Zechariah, who lived when Herod was king of Judea. Zechariah was a member of the priestly order of Abijah. His wife, Elizabeth, was also from the priestly line of Aaron. Zechariah and Elizabeth were righteous in God's eyes, careful to obey all of the Lord's commandments and regulations. They had no children because Elizabeth was barren, and now they were both very old ...

But the angel said, "Don't be afraid, Zechariah! For God has heard your prayer, and your wife, Elizabeth, will bear you a son! And you are to name him John ...

Soon afterward his wife, Elizabeth, became pregnant and went into seclusion for five months ...

In the sixth month of Elizabeth's pregnancy, God sent the angel Gabriel to Nazareth, a village in Galilee ...(to Mary)

What's more, your relative Elizabeth has become pregnant in her old age! People used to say she was barren, but she's already in her sixth month ...

A few days later Mary hurried to the hill country of Judea, to the town where Zechariah lived. She entered the house and greeted Elizabeth. At the sound of Mary's greeting, Elizabeth's child leaped within her, and Elizabeth was filled with the Holy Spirit...

Elizabeth gave a glad cry and exclaimed to Mary, "You are blessed by God above all other women, and your child is blessed. ...

Mary stayed with Elizabeth about three months and then went back to her own home ...

Now it was time for Elizabeth's baby to be born, and it was a boy. When the baby was eight days old, all the relatives and friends came for the circumcision ceremony. They wanted to name him Zechariah, after his father.

But Elizabeth said, "No! His name is John!" ...

Euodia and Syntyche

Philippians 4:1-3 KJV

Therefore, my brethren dearly beloved and longed for, my joy and crown, so stand fast in the Lord, *my* dearly beloved. I beseech Euodias, and beseech Syntyche, that they be of the same mind in the Lord. And I entreat thee also, true yokefellow, help those women which laboured with me in the gospel, with Clement also, and *with* other my fellowlabourers, whose names *are* in the book of life.

Herodias, Salome (#1) and the Beheading of John the Baptist

Mark 6:17-29 KJV

For Herod himself had sent forth and laid hold upon John, and bound him in prison for Herodias' sake, his brother Philip's wife: for he had married her.

For John had said unto Herod, It is not lawful for thee to have thy brother's wife.

Therefore Herodias had a quarrel against him, and would have killed him; but she could not:

For Herod feared John, knowing that he was a just man and an holy, and observed him; and when he heard him, he did many things, and heard him gladly.

And when a convenient day was come, that Herod on his birthday made a supper to his lords, high captains, and chief estates of Galilee;

And when the daughter [Salome] of the said Herodias came in, and danced, and pleased Herod and them that sat with him, the king said unto the damsel, Ask of me whatsoever thou wilt, and I will give it thee.

And he sware unto her, Whatsoever thou shalt ask of me, I will give it thee, unto the half of my kingdom.

And she went forth, and said unto her mother, What shall I ask? And she said, The head of John the Baptist.

And she came in straightway with haste unto the king, and asked, saying, I will that thou give me by and by in a charger the head of John the Baptist.

And the king was exceeding sorry; yet for his oath's sake, and for their sakes which sat with him, he would not reject her.

And immediately the king sent an executioner, and commanded his head to be brought:and he went and beheaded him in the prison,

And brought his head in a charger, and gave it to the damsel: and the damsel gave it to her mother.

And when his disciples heard of it, they came and took up his corpse, and laid it in a tomb.

Jairus' Daughter

Mark 5:21-24 KJV

And when Jesus was passed over again by ship unto the other side, much people gathered unto him: and he was nigh unto the sea. And, behold, there cometh one of the rulers of the synagogue, Jairus by name; and when he saw him, he fell at his feet, And besought him greatly, saying, My little daughter lieth at the point of death: *I pray thee*, come and lay thy hands on her, that she may be healed; and she shall live. And *Jesus* went with him; and much people followed him, and thronged him.

Mark 5:35-42 NLT

While he was still speaking to her, messengers arrived from Jairus's home with the message, "Your daughter is dead. There's no use troubling the Teacher now."

But Jesus ignored their comments and said to Jairus, "Don't be afraid. Just trust me." Then Jesus stopped the crowd and wouldn't let anyone go with him except Peter and James and John. When they came to the home of the synagogue leader, Jesus saw the commotion and the weeping and wailing. He went inside and spoke to the people. "Why all this weeping and commotion?" he asked. "The child isn't dead; she is only asleep."

The crowd laughed at him, but he told them all to go outside. Then he took the girl's father and mother and his three disciples into the room where the girl was lying. Holding her hand, he said to her, "Get up, little girl!" And the girl, who was twelve years old, immediately stood up and walked around! Her parents were absolutely overwhelmed.

Jesus' Sisters

Mark 6:1-6 NIV

Jesus left there and went to his hometown, accompanied by his disciples. When the Sabbath came, he began to teach in the synagogue, and many who heard him were amazed.

"Where did this man get these things?" they asked. "What's this wisdom that has been given him, that he even does miracles! Isn't this the carpenter? Isn't this Mary's son and the brother of James, Joseph, Judas and Simon? Aren't his sisters here with us?" And they took offense at him.

Jesus said to them, "Only in his hometown, among his relatives and in his own house is a prophet without honor." He could not do any miracles there, except lay his hands on a few sick people and heal them. And he was amazed at their lack of faith.

Matthew 13:55-56 NLT

When Jesus had finished telling these stories, he left that part of the country. He returned to Nazareth, his hometown. When he taught there in the synagogue, everyone was astonished and said, "Where does he get his wisdom and his miracles? He's just a carpenter's son, and we know Mary, his mother, and his brothers—James, Joseph, Simon, and Judas. All his sisters live right here among us. What makes him so great?" And they were deeply offended and refused to believe in him.

Then Jesus told them, "A prophet is honored everywhere except in his own hometown and among his own family." And so he did only a few miracles there because of their unbelief.

Joanna, Susanna & Mary(s) (Women With Jesus)

Luke 8:1-3 NLT

Not long afterward Jesus began a tour of the nearby cities and villages to announce the Good News concerning the Kingdom of God. He took his twelve disciples with him, along with some women he had healed and from whom he had cast out evil spirits. Among them were Mary Magdalene, from whom he had cast out seven demons; Joanna, the wife of Chuza, Herod's business manager; Susanna; and many others who were contributing from their own resources to support Jesus and his disciples.

Luke 23:55-56 NIV

The women who had come with Jesus from Galilee followed Joseph and saw the tomb and how his body was laid in it. Then they went home and prepared spices and perfumes. But they rested on the Sabbath in obedience to the commandment.

John 19:25 NIV)

Near the cross of Jesus stood his mother, his mother's sister, Mary the wife of Clopas, and Mary Magdalene.

Mark 15:40-41 NIV

Some women were watching from a distance. Among them were Mary Magdalene, Mary the mother of James the younger and of Joses, and Salome. In Galilee these women had followed him and cared for his needs. Many other women who had come up with him to Jerusalem were also there.

Luke 24:1-3, 8-10, 18, 25-26, 31 KJV

Now upon the first *day* of the week, very early in the morning, they came unto the sepulchre, bringing the spices which they had prepared, and certain *others* with them. And they found the stone rolled away from the sepulchre. And they entered in, and found not the body of the Lord Jesus ... And they remembered his words, And returned from the sepulchre, and told all these things unto the eleven, and to all the rest. It was Mary Magdalene, and Joanna, and Mary *the mother* of James, and other *women that were* with them, which told these things unto the apostles ... And it came to pass, that, while they communed *together* and reasoned, Jesus himself drew near, and went with them ... And the one of them, whose name was Cleopas, answering said unto him, Art thou only a stranger in Jerusalem, and hast not known the things which are come to pass there in these days ... Then he said unto them, O fools, and slow of heart to believe all that the prophets have spoken: Ought not Christ to have suffered these things, and to enter into his glory ... And their eyes were opened, and they knew him ...

Lois and Eunice

Acts 16:1 AMP

And [Paul] went down to Derbe and also to Lystra. A disciple named Timothy was there, the son of a Jewish woman who was a believer [she had become convinced that Jesus is the Messiah and the Author of eternal salvation, and yielded obedience to Him]; but [Timothy's] father was a Greek.

II Timothy 1:5-7; 3:14-15 NIV

I have been reminded of your sincere faith, which first lived in your grandmother Lois and in your mother Eunice and, I am persuaded, now lives in you also. For this reason I remind you to fan into flame the gift of God, which is in you through the laying on of my hands. For God did not give us a spirit of timidity, but a spirit of power, of love and of self-discipline.

But as for you, continue in what you have learned and have become convinced of, because you know those from whom you learned it, and how from infancy you have known the holy Scriptures, which are able to make you wise for salvation through faith in Christ Jesus.

Lydia

Acts 16:14-15, 40 KJV

And a certain woman named Lydia, a seller of purple, of the city of Thyatira, which worshipped God, heard *us*: whose heart the Lord opened, that she attended unto the things which were spoken of Paul. And when she was baptized, and her household, she besought *us*, saying, If ye have judged me to be faithful to the Lord, come into my house, and abide *there*. And she constrained us.

... And they went out of the prison, and entered into *the house of* Lydia: and when they had seen the brethren, they comforted them, and departed.

Mary and Martha: Only One Thing Is Needed

Luke 10:38-42 NLT

As Jesus and the disciples continued on their way to Jerusalem, they came to a village where a woman named Martha welcomed them into her home.

Her sister, Mary, sat at the Lord's feet, listening to what he taught.

But Martha was worrying over the big dinner she was preparing. She came to Jesus and said, "Lord, doesn't it seem unfair to you that my sister just sits here while I do all the work? Tell her to come and help me."

But the Lord said to her, "My dear Martha, you are so upset over all these details!

There is really only one thing worth being concerned about. Mary has discovered it--and I won't take it away from her."

Mary and Martha with Lazarus

John 11:20-39 NIV

When Martha heard that Jesus was coming, she went out to meet him, but Mary stayed at home.

"Lord," Martha said to Jesus, "if you had been here, my brother would not have died. But I know that even now God will give you whatever you ask."

Jesus said to her, "Your brother will rise again."

Martha answered, "I know he will rise again in the resurrection at the last day."

Jesus said to her, "I am the resurrection and the life. He who believes in me will live, even though he dies; and whoever lives and believes in me will never die. Do you believe this?"

"Yes, Lord," she told him, "I believe that you are the Christ, the Son of God, who was to come into the world."

And after she had said this, she went back and called her sister Mary aside. "The Teacher is here," she said, "and is asking for you." When Mary heard this, she got up quickly and went to him. Now Jesus had not yet entered the village, but was still at the place where Martha had met him. When the Jews who had been with Mary in the house, comforting her, noticed how quickly she got up and went out, they followed her, supposing she was going to the tomb to mourn there.

When Mary reached the place where Jesus was and saw him, she fell at his feet and said, "Lord, if you had been here, my brother would not have died." When Jesus saw her weeping, and the Jews who had come along with her also weeping, he was deeply moved in spirit and troubled. "Where have you laid him?" he asked.

"Come and see, Lord," they replied.

Jesus wept.

Then the Jews said, "See how he loved him!"

But some of them said, "Could not he who opened the eyes of the blind man have kept this man from dying?"

Jesus, once more deeply moved, came to the tomb. It was a cave with a stone laid across the entrance. "Take away the stone," he said.

"But, Lord," said Martha, the sister of the dead man, "by this time there is a bad odor, for he has been there four days."

Mary Anoints Jesus,
(Woman with Alabaster Box)

John 11:2 KJV

It was ... Mary which anointed the Lord with ointment, and wiped his feet with her hair.

Matthew 26:7-13 KJV

There came unto him a woman having an alabaster box of very precious ointment, and poured it on his head, as he sat at meat.

But when his disciples saw it, they had indignation, saying, To what purpose is this waste? For this ointment might have been sold for much, and given to the poor.

When Jesus understood it, he said unto them, Why trouble ye the woman? for she hath wrought a good work upon me. For ye have the poor always with you; but me ye have not always.

For in that she hath poured this ointment on my body, she did it for my burial. Verily I say unto you, Wheresoever this gospel shall be preached in the whole world, there shall also this, that this woman hath done, be told for a memorial of her.

Matthew 26:7-13 NIV

... a woman came to him with an alabaster jar of very expensive perfume, which she poured on his head as he was reclining at the table. When the disciples saw this, they were indignant. "Why this waste?" they asked. "This perfume could have been sold at a high price and the money given to the poor."

Aware of this, Jesus said to them, "Why are you bothering this woman? She has done a beautiful thing to me. The poor you will always have with you, but you will not always have me. When she poured this perfume on my body, she did it to prepare me for burial. I tell you the truth, wherever this gospel is preached throughout the world, what she has done will also be told, in memory of her."

Mary Magdalene

Luke 8:1-2 KJV
(Her Deliverance)

And it came to pass afterward, that he went throughout every city and village, preaching and shewing the glad tidings of the kingdom of God:and the twelve were with him, And certain women, which had been healed of evil spirits and infirmities, Mary called Magdalene, out of whom went seven devils ...

Matthew 27:55-56 KJV
(At the Crucifixion and Burial of Jesus)

And many women were there beholding afar off, which followed Jesus from Galilee, ministering unto him: Among which was Mary Magdalene ...

John 20:2, 11-18 KJV
(The First to See That Jesus Had Risen)

The first day of the week cometh Mary Magdalene early, when it was yet dark, unto the sepulchre, and seeth the stone taken away from the sepulchre. Then she runneth, and cometh to Simon Peter, and to the other disciple, whom Jesus loved, and saith unto them, They have taken away the LORD out of the sepulchre, and we know not where they have laid him. Then the disciples went away again unto their own home. But Mary stood without at the sepulchre weeping: and as she wept, she stooped down, and looked into the sepulchre, And seeth two angels in white sitting, the one at the head, and the other at the feet, where the body of Jesus had lain. And they say unto her, Woman, why weepest thou? She saith unto them, Because they have taken away my LORD, and I know not where they have laid him.

And when she had thus said, she turned herself back, and saw Jesus standing, and knew not that it was Jesus.

Jesus saith unto her, Woman, why weepest thou? whom seekest thou? She, supposing him to be the gardener, saith unto him, Sir, if thou have borne him hence, tell me where thou hast laid him, and I will take him away.

Jesus saith unto her, Mary. She turned herself, and saith unto him, Rabboni; which is to say, Master.

Jesus saith unto her, Touch me not; for I am not yet ascended to my Father: but go to my brethren, and say unto them, I ascend unto my Father, and your Father; and to my God, and your God.

Mary Magdalene came and told the disciples that she had seen the LORD, and that he had spoken these things unto her.

Mary, Mother of James and Joses

Mark 15:37-41 NLT

Then Jesus uttered another loud cry and breathed his last. And the curtain in the Temple was torn in two, from top to bottom. When the Roman officer who stood facing him saw how he had died, he exclaimed, "Truly, this was the Son of God!"

Some women were there, watching from a distance, including Mary Magdalene, Mary (the mother of James the younger and of Joseph), and Salome. They had been followers of Jesus and had cared for him while he was in Galilee. Then they and many other women had come with him to Jerusalem.

Matthew 27:59-61; 28:1-10 NIV

Joseph took the body, wrapped it in a clean linen cloth, and placed it in his own new tomb that he had cut out of the rock. He rolled a big stone in front of the entrance to the tomb and went away. Mary Magdalene and the other Mary were sitting there opposite the tomb.

After the Sabbath, at dawn on the first day of the week, Mary Magdalene and the other Mary went to look at the tomb.

There was a violent earthquake, for an angel of the Lord came down from heaven and, going to the tomb, rolled back the stone and sat on it. His appearance was like lightning, and his clothes were white as snow. The guards were so afraid of him that they shook and became like dead men.

The angel said to the women, "Do not be afraid, for I know that you are looking for Jesus, who was crucified. He is not here; he has risen, just as he said. Come and see the place where he lay. Then go quickly and tell his disciples:'He has risen from the dead and is going ahead of you into Galilee. There you will see him.' Now I have told you."

So the women hurried away from the tomb, afraid yet filled with joy, and ran to tell his disciples. Suddenly Jesus met them. "Greetings," he said. They came to him, clasped his feet and worshiped him. Then Jesus said to them, "Do not be afraid. Go and tell my brothers to go to Galilee; there they will see me."

Luke 24:9-12 KJV

And returned from the sepulchre, and told all these things unto the eleven, and to all the rest. It was Mary Magdalene, and Joanna, and Mary *the mother* of James, and other *women that were* with them, which told these things unto the apostles. And their words seemed to them as idle tales, and they believed them not. Then arose Peter, and ran unto the sepulchre; and stooping down, he beheld the linen clothes laid by themselves, and departed, wondering in himself at that which was come to pass.

Mary, Mother of Jesus

Matthew 1:18-25 NLT

Now this is how Jesus the Messiah was born. His mother, Mary, was engaged to be married to Joseph. But while she was still a virgin, she became pregnant by the Holy Spirit. Joseph, her fiance, being a just man, decided to break the engagement quietly, so as not to disgrace her publicly.

As he considered this, he fell asleep, and an angel of the Lord appeared to him in a dream. "Joseph, son of David," the angel said, "do not be afraid to go ahead with your marriage to Mary. For the child within her has been conceived by the Holy Spirit. And she will have a son, and you are to name him Jesus, for he will save his people from their sins." All of this happened to fulfill the Lord's message through his prophet:

"Look! The virgin will conceive a child!

She will give birth to a son,

and he will be called Immanuel (meaning, God is with us)."

When Joseph woke up, he did what the angel of the Lord commanded. He brought Mary home to be his wife, but she remained a virgin until her son was born. And Joseph named him Jesus.

Matthew 13:55 NIV

"Isn't this the carpenter's son? Isn't his mother's name Mary, and aren't his brothers James, Joseph, Simon and Judas? Aren't all his sisters with us?

Luke 2:13-19 KJV

And suddenly there was with the angel a multitude of the heavenly host praising God, and saying, Glory to God in the highest, and on earth peace, good will toward men.

And it came to pass, as the angels were gone away from them into heaven, the shepherds said one to another, Let us now go even unto Bethlehem, and see this thing which is come to pass, which the Lord hath made known unto us.

And they came with haste, and found Mary, and Joseph, and the babe lying in a manger ...

But Mary kept all these things, and pondered them in her heart.

John 19:25 KJV

Now there stood by the cross of Jesus his mother, and his mother's sister, Mary the wife of Cleophas, and Mary Magdalene.

Mary, Mother of Mark John, with Rhoda

Acts 12:11-16 KJV

And when Peter was come to himself, he said, Now I know of a surety, that the Lord hath sent his angel, and hath delivered me out of the hand of Herod, and *from* all the expectation of the people of the Jews. And when he had considered *the thing*, he came to the house of Mary the mother of John, whose surname was Mark; where many were gathered together praying. And as Peter knocked at the door of the gate, a damsel came to hearken, named Rhoda. And when she knew Peter's voice, she opened not the gate for gladness, but ran in, and told how Peter stood before the gate. And they said unto her, Thou art mad. But she constantly affirmed that it was even so. Then said they, It is his angel. But Peter continued knocking:

and when they had opened *the door*, and saw him, they were astonished.

Persistent Widow

Luke 18:1-8 KJV

And he spake a parable unto them *to this end*, that men ought always to pray, and not to faint; Saying, There was in a city a judge, which feared not God, neither regarded man: And there was a widow in that city; and she came unto him, saying, Avenge me of mine adversary. And he would not for a while: but afterward he said within himself, Though I fear not God, nor regard man; Yet because this widow troubleth me, I will avenge her, lest by her continual coming she weary me. And the Lord said, Hear what the unjust judge saith. And shall not God avenge his own elect, which cry day and night unto him, though he bear long with them? I tell you that he will avenge them speedily. Nevertheless when the Son of man cometh, shall he find faith on the earth?

Peter's Mother-In-Law

Matthew 8:14-15 KJV

And when Jesus was come into Peter's house, he saw his wife's mother laid, and sick of a fever.

And he touched her hand, and the fever left her: and she arose, and ministered unto them.

Phebe

Romans 16:1-2 KJV

I commend unto you Phebe our sister, which is a servant of the church which is at Cenchrea: That ye receive her in the Lord, as becometh saints, and that ye assist her in whatsoever business she hath need of you: for she hath been a succourer of many, and of myself also.

Pilate's Wife

Matthew 27:19 KJV

When he was set down on the judgment seat, his wife sent unto him, saying, Have thou nothing to do with that just man: for I have suffered many things this day in a dream because of him.

Priscilla

Acts 18:1-5, 12-13, 18, 24-26 KJV

After these things Paul departed from Athens, and came to Corinth; And found a certain Jew named Aquila, born in Pontus, lately come from Italy, with his wife Priscilla; (because that Claudius had commanded all Jews to depart from Rome) and came unto them.

And because he was of the same craft, he abode with them, and wrought: for by their occupation they were tentmakers. And he reasoned in the synagogue every sabbath, and persuaded the Jews and the Greeks.

And when Silas and Timotheus were come from Macedonia, Paul was pressed in the spirit, and testified to the Jews that Jesus was Christ.

… the Jews made insurrection with one accord against Paul, and brought him to the judgment seat, Saying, This fellow persuadeth men to worship God contrary to the law.

And Paul after this tarried there yet a good while, and then took his leave of the brethren, and sailed thence into Syria, and with him Priscilla and Aquila; having shorn his head in Cenchrea:for he had a vow.

And a certain Jew named Apollos, born at Alexandria, an eloquent man, and mighty in the scriptures, came to Ephesus.

This man was instructed in the way of the Lord; and being fervent in the spirit, he spake and taught diligently the things of the Lord, knowing only the baptism of John.

And he began to speak boldly in the synagogue: whom when Aquila and Priscilla had heard, they took him unto them, and expounded unto him the way of God more perfectly.

Roman 16:3-4 KJV

Greet Priscilla and Aquila my helpers in Christ Jesus: Who have for my life laid down their own necks: unto whom not only I give thanks, but also all the churches of the Gentiles.

1 Corinthians 16:19-21 KJV

The churches of Asia salute you. Aquila and Priscilla salute you much in the Lord, with the church that is in their house. All the brethren greet you. Greet ye one another with an holy kiss. The salutation of me Paul with mine own hand.

Salome (#2), Mother of Zebedee's Children

Matthew 20:20-24 KJV

Then came to him the mother of Zebedee's children with her sons, worshipping *him*, and desiring a certain thing of him. And he said unto her, What wilt thou? She saith unto him, Grant that these my two sons may sit, the one on thy right hand, and the other on the left, in thy kingdom. But Jesus answered and said, Ye know not what ye ask. Are ye able to drink of the cup that I shall drink of, and to be baptized with the baptism that I am baptized with? They say unto him, We are able. And he saith unto them, Ye shall drink indeed of my cup, and be baptized with the baptism that I am baptized with: but to sit on my right hand, and on my left, is not mine to give, but *it shall be given to them* for whom it is prepared of my Father. And when the ten heard *it*, they were moved with indignation against the two brethren.

Mark 15:37-41 NLT

Then Jesus uttered another loud cry and breathed his last. And the curtain in the Temple was torn in two, from top to bottom. When the Roman officer who stood facing him saw how he had died, he exclaimed, "Truly, this was the Son of God!"

Some women were there, watching from a distance, including Mary Magdalene, Mary (the mother of James the younger and of Joseph), and Salome. They had been followers of Jesus and had cared for him while he was in Galilee. Then they and many other women had come with him to Jerusalem.

Mark 16:1-6 NIV

When the Sabbath was over, Mary Magdalene, Mary the mother of James, and Salome bought spices so that they might go to anoint Jesus' body. Very early on the first day of the week, just after sunrise, they were on their way to the tomb and they asked each other, "Who will roll the stone away from the entrance of the tomb?"

But when they looked up, they saw that the stone, which was very large, had been rolled away.[5]As they entered the tomb, they saw a young man dressed in a white robe sitting on the right side, and they were alarmed.

"Don't be alarmed," he said. "You are looking for Jesus the Nazarene, who was crucified. He has risen! He is not here …"

Samaritan Women by Jacob's Well

John 4:4-26 NIV

So he came to a town in Samaria called Sychar, near the plot of ground Jacob had given to his son Joseph. Jacob's well was there, and Jesus, tired as he was from the journey, sat down by the well. It was about the sixth hour.

When a Samaritan woman came to draw water, Jesus said to her, "Will you give me a drink?" (His disciples had gone into the town to buy food.) The Samaritan woman said to him, "You are a Jew and I am a Samaritan woman. How can you ask me for a drink?" (For Jews do not associate with Samaritans.)

Jesus answered her, "If you knew the gift of God and who it is that asks you for a drink, you would have asked him and he would have given you living water."

"Sir," the woman said, "you have nothing to draw with and the well is deep. Where can you get this living water? Are you greater than our father Jacob, who gave us the well and drank from it himself, as did also his sons and his flocks and herds?"

Jesus answered, "Everyone who drinks this water will be thirsty again, but whoever drinks the water I give him will never thirst. Indeed, the water I give him will become in him a spring of water welling up to eternal life."

The woman said to him, "Sir, give me this water so that I won't get thirsty and have to keep coming here to draw water."

He told her, "Go, call your husband and come back."

"I have no husband," she replied.

Jesus said to her, "You are right when you say you have no husband. The fact is, you have had five husbands, and the man you now have is not your husband. What you have just said is quite true."

"Sir," the woman said, "I can see that you are a prophet. Our fathers worshiped on this mountain, but you Jews claim that the place where we must worship is in Jerusalem."

Jesus declared, "Believe me, woman, a time is coming when you will worship the Father neither on this mountain nor in Jerusalem. You Samaritans worship what you do not know; we worship what we do know, for salvation is from the Jews. Yet a time is coming and has now come when the true worshipers will worship the Father in spirit and truth, for they are the kind of worshipers the Father seeks. God is spirit, and his worshipers must worship in spirit and in truth."

The woman said, "I know that Messiah" (called Christ) "is coming. When he comes, he will explain everything to us."

Then Jesus declared, "I who speak to you am he."

Sapphira, Ananias' Wife

Acts 5:1-11 AMP

But A certain man named Ananias with his wife Sapphira sold a piece of property,

And with his wife's knowledge and connivance he kept back and wrongfully appropriated some of the proceeds, bringing only a part and putting it at the feet of the apostles.

But Peter said, Ananias, why has Satan filled your heart that you should lie to and attempt to deceive the Holy Spirit, and should [in violation of your promise] withdraw secretly and appropriate to your own use part of the price from the sale of the land?

As long as it remained unsold, was it not still your own? And [even] after it was sold, was not [the money] at your disposal and under your control? Why then, is it that you have proposed and purposed in your heart to do this thing? [How could you have the heart to do such a deed?] You have not [simply] lied to men [playing false and showing yourself utterly deceitful] but to God.

Upon hearing these words, Ananias fell down and died. And great dread and terror took possession of all who heard of it. And the young men arose and wrapped up [the body] and carried it out and buried it.

Now after an interval of about three hours his wife came in, not having learned of what had happened.

And Peter said to her, Tell me, did you sell the land for so much? Yes, she said, for so much.

Then Peter said to her, How could you two have agreed and conspired together to try to deceive the Spirit of the Lord? Listen! The feet of those who have buried your husband are at the door, and they will carry you out [also].

And instantly she fell down at his feet and died; and the young men entering found her dead, and they carried her out and buried her beside her husband.

And the whole church and all others who heard of these things were appalled [great awe and strange terror and dread seized them].

Ten Virgins

Matthew 25:1-13 KJV

Then shall the kingdom of heaven be likened unto ten virgins, which took their lamps, and went forth to meet the bridegroom. And five of them were wise, and five *were* foolish. They that *were* foolish took their lamps, and took no oil with them: But the wise took oil in their vessels with their lamps. While the bridegroom tarried, they all slumbered and slept. And at midnight there was a cry made, Behold, the bridegroom cometh; go ye out to meet him. Then all those virgins arose, and trimmed their lamps. And the foolish said unto the wise, Give us of your oil; for our lamps are gone out. But the wise answered, saying, *Not so*; lest there be not enough for us and you: but go ye rather to them that sell, and buy for yourselves. And while they went to buy, the bridegroom came; and they that were ready went in with him to the marriage: and the door was shut. Afterward came also the other virgins, saying, Lord, Lord, open to us. But he answered and said, Verily I say unto you, I know you not. Watch therefore, for ye know neither the day nor the hour wherein the Son of man cometh.

Widow Who Gave Two Mites

Mark 12:41-44 KJV

And Jesus sat over against the treasury, and beheld how the people cast money into the treasury: and many that were rich cast in much. And there came a certain poor widow, and she threw in two mites, which make a farthing. And he called *unto him* his disciples, and saith unto them, Verily I say unto you, That this poor widow hath cast more in, than all they which have cast into the treasury: For all *they* did cast in of their abundance; but she of her want did cast in all that she had, *even* all her living.

Luke 21:1-4 NIV

As he looked up, Jesus saw the rich putting their gifts into the temple treasury. He also saw a poor widow put in two very small copper coins. "I tell you the truth," he said, "this poor widow has put in more than all the others. All these people gave their gifts out of their wealth; but she out of her poverty put in all she had to live on."

Luke 21:1-4 NLT

While Jesus was in the Temple, he watched the rich people putting their gifts into the collection box. Then a poor widow came by and dropped in two pennies. "I assure you," he said, "this poor widow has given more than all the rest of them. For they have given a tiny part of their surplus, but she, poor as she is, has given everything she has."

Woman Caught In Adultery

John 8:1-11 NLT

Jesus returned to the Mount of Olives, but early the next morning he was back again at the Temple. A crowd soon gathered, and he sat down and taught them. As he was speaking, the teachers of religious law and Pharisees brought a woman they had caught in the act of adultery. They put her in front of the crowd.

"Teacher," they said to Jesus, "this woman was caught in the very act of adultery. The law of Moses says to stone her. What do you say?"

They were trying to trap him into saying something they could use against him, but Jesus stooped down and wrote in the dust with his finger. They kept demanding an answer, so he stood up again and said, "All right, stone her. But let those who have never sinned throw the first stones!" Then he stooped down again and wrote in the dust.

When the accusers heard this, they slipped away one by one, beginning with the oldest, until only Jesus was left in the middle of the crowd with the woman. Then Jesus stood up again and said to her, "Where are your accusers? Didn't even one of them condemn you?"

"No, Lord," she said.

And Jesus said, "Neither do I. Go and sin no more."

Woman Clothed With the Sun

Revelations 12:1-17

And there appeared a great wonder in heaven; a woman clothed with the sun, and the moon under her feet, and upon her head a crown of twelve stars:

And she being with child cried, travailing in birth, and pained to be delivered.

And there appeared another wonder in heaven; and behold a great red dragon, having seven heads and ten horns, and seven crowns upon his heads.

And his tail drew the third part of the stars of heaven, and did cast them to the earth: and the dragon stood before the woman which was ready to be delivered, for to devour her child as soon as it was born.

And she brought forth a man child, who was to rule all nations with a rod of iron: and her child was caught up unto God, and to his throne.

And the woman fled into the wilderness, where she hath a place prepared of God, that they should feed her there a thousand two hundred and threescore days.

And there was war in heaven: Michael and his angels fought against the dragon; and the dragon fought and his angels,

And prevailed not; neither was their place found any more in heaven.

And the great dragon was cast out, that old serpent, called the Devil, and Satan, which deceiveth the whole world: he was cast out into the earth, and his angels were cast out with him.

And I heard a loud voice saying in heaven, Now is come salvation, and strength, and the kingdom of our God, and the power of his Christ: for the accuser of our brethren is cast down, which accused them before our God day and night.

And they overcame him by the blood of the Lamb, and by the word of their testimony; and they loved not their lives unto the death.

Therefore rejoice, ye heavens, and ye that dwell in them. Woe to the inhabiters of the earth and of the sea! for the devil is come down unto you, having great wrath, because he knoweth that he hath but a short time.

And when the dragon saw that he was cast unto the earth, he persecuted the woman which brought forth the man child.

And to the woman were given two wings of a great eagle, that she might fly into the wilderness, into her place, where she is nourished for a time, and times, and half a time, from the face of the serpent.

And the serpent cast out of his mouth water as a flood after the woman, that he might cause her to be carried away of the flood.

And the earth helped the woman, and the earth opened her mouth, and swallowed up the flood which the dragon cast out of his mouth.

And the dragon was wroth with the woman, and went to make war with the remnant of her seed, which keep the commandments of God, and have the testimony of Jesus Christ.

Woman Who Begged For Daughter's Healing

Matthew 15:22-28 KJV

Then Jesus went thence, and departed into the coasts of Tyre and Sidon. And, behold, a woman of Canaan came out of the same coasts, and cried unto him, saying, Have mercy on me, O Lord, *thou* Son of David; my daughter is grievously vexed with a devil. But he answered her not a word. And his disciples came and besought him, saying, Send her away; for she crieth after us. But he answered and said, I am not sent but unto the lost sheep of the house of Israel. Then came she and worshipped him, saying, Lord, help me. But he answered and said, It is not meet to take the children's bread, and to cast *it* to dogs. And she said, Truth, Lord: yet the dogs eat of the crumbs which fall from their masters' table. Then Jesus answered and said unto her, O woman, great *is* thy faith: be it unto thee even as thou wilt. And her daughter was made whole from that very hour.

Mark 7:24-30 NLT

Then Jesus left Galilee and went north to the region of Tyre. He tried to keep it secret that he was there, but he couldn't. As usual, the news of his arrival spread fast. Right away a woman came to him whose little girl was possessed by an evil spirit. She had heard about Jesus, and now she came and fell at his feet. She begged him to release her child from the demon's control.

Since she was a Gentile, born in Syrian Phoenicia, Jesus told her, "First I should help my own family, the Jews. It isn't right to take food from the children and throw it to the dogs."

She replied, "That's true, Lord, but even the dogs under the table are given some crumbs from the children's plates."

"Good answer!" he said. "And because you have answered so well, I have healed your daughter." And when she arrived home, her little girl was lying quietly in bed, and the demon was gone.

Woman With the Issue of Blood

Mark 5:25-34 KJV

And a certain woman, which had an issue of blood twelve years,

And had suffered many things of many physicians, and had spent all that she had, and was nothing bettered, but rather grew worse,

When she had heard of Jesus, came in the press behind, and touched his garment.

For she said, If I may touch but his clothes, I shall be whole.

And straightway the fountain of her blood was dried up; and she felt in her body that she was healed of that plague.

And Jesus, immediately knowing in himself that virtue had gone out of him, turned him about in the press, and said, Who touched my clothes?

And his disciples said unto him, Thou seest the multitude thronging thee, and sayest thou, Who touched me?

And he looked round about to see her that had done this thing.

But the woman fearing and trembling, knowing what was done in her, came and fell down before him, and told him all the truth.

And he said unto her, Daughter, thy faith hath made thee whole; go in peace, and be whole of thy plague.

Joanna, Susanna & Mary(s)
(Women With Jesus)

Luke 8:1-3 NLT

Not long afterward Jesus began a tour of the nearby cities and villages to announce the Good News concerning the Kingdom of God. He took his twelve disciples with him, along with some women he had healed and from whom he had cast out evil spirits. Among them were Mary Magdalene, from whom he had cast out seven demons; Joanna, the wife of Chuza, Herod's business manager; Susanna; and many others who were contributing from their own resources to support Jesus and his disciples.

Luke 23:55-56 NIV

The women who had come with Jesus from Galilee followed Joseph and saw the tomb and how his body was laid in it. Then they went home and prepared spices and perfumes. But they rested on the Sabbath in obedience to the commandment.

John 19:25 NIV)

Near the cross of Jesus stood his mother, his mother's sister, Mary the wife of Clopas, and Mary Magdalene.

Mark 15:40-41 NIV

Some women were watching from a distance. Among them were Mary Magdalene, Mary the mother of James the younger and of Joses, and Salome. In Galilee these women had followed him and cared for his needs. Many other women who had come up with him to Jerusalem were also there.

Luke 24:13, 8-10, 18, 25-26, 31 KJV

Now upon the first *day* of the week, very early in the morning, they came unto the sepulchre, bringing the spices which they had prepared, and certain *others* with them. And they found the stone rolled away from the sepulchre. And they entered in, and found not the body of the Lord Jesus ... And they remembered his words, And returned from the sepulchre, and told all these things unto the eleven, and to all the rest. It was Mary Magdalene, and Joanna, and Mary *the mother* of James, and other *women that were* with them, which told these things unto the apostles ... And it came to pass, that, while they communed *together* and reasoned, Jesus himself drew near, and went with them ... And the one of them, whose name was Cleopas, answering said unto him, Art thou only a stranger in Jerusalem, and hast not known the things which are come to pass there in these days ... Then he said unto them, O fools, and slow of heart to believe all that the prophets have spoken:Ought not Christ to have suffered these things, and to enter into his glory ... And their eyes were opened, and they knew him ...

Do You Have a Relationship With God?

The Bible tells us that:

> *... if you confess with your mouth, "Jesus is Lord," and believe in your heart that God raised him from the dead, you will be saved.*

Romans 10:9 KJV

HAVE YOU ACCEPTED JESUS AS YOUR LORD?

If you do not have a relationship with God – through accepting Jesus as Lord – then I invite you to please pray the following prayer:

Lord, I come before you today to confess that I accept Jesus as my Lord and Savior and that I believe you raised Him from the dead. I believe that He died for my sins and that only through Him can I be saved.

Lord, please forgive me of all my sins and accept me into your Kingdom. Lord, I welcome the Holy Spirit into my heart today.

I thank you, Lord, in Jesus' Name, Amen.

Congratulations! Now, you - as a born-again Christian can best maintain your walk with God by:

- Praying daily – ask God to help you with the challenges in your life and to bring you closer to Himself
- Read and Study God's Word (the Bible) daily
- Attend a Bible teaching church
- Fellowship with other serious Christians

A good place to start your Bible reading is with the book of John.

If you have questions or need help please write to me at:

Akili Kumasi
GOD IS LOVE MINISTRIES
P.O. Box 80275, Brooklyn, NY 11208
kumasi@GILpublications.com

Mail Order ....GIL Publications
P. O. Box 80275, Brooklyn, NY 11208
Telephone Orders................(718) 386-6434
Website Orders ....www.GILpublications.com

SCRIPTURE REFERENCE BOOKS			
Book Title	Price	#	Total
God's Healing Scriptures 240 Prayers & Promises in the Bible	$9.95		
101 Women in the Bible	$6.95		
101 Prayers in the Bible	$6.95		
101 Victories in the Bible	$6.95		
HALL OF FAITH CLASSICS			
Volume 1: The Person and Work of the Holy Spirit (R.A. Torrey)	$9.75		
Volume 2: How to Pray (R.A. Torrey)	$5.95		
Volume 3: How To Obtain the Fullness of Power for Life and Christian Service (R.A. Torrey)	$5.75		
Volume 4: Absolute Surrender (Andrew Murray)	$6.25		
Volume 5: Humility: The Beauty of Holiness (Andrew Murray)	$5.75		
Hall of Faith 5-Pack (Volumes 1, 2, 3, 4, 5) - $25% off – Save $8.35	$25.10		
FATHERHOOD BOOKS			
Fatherhood Principles of Joseph the Carpenter	$8.95		
Fun Meals for Fathers and Sons	$4.95		
On the Outside Looking In	$7.95		

To pay by Credit / Debit Card – go to www.GILpublications.com or call 718-386-6434

Complete the Order Form on the next page

Mail Order .... GIL Publications
P. O. Box 80275, Brooklyn, NY 11208
Telephone Orders .... (718) 386-6434
Website Orders .... www.GILpublications.com

Book Title	Price	#	Total
Bible Word Search – Puzzles with Scriptures (80 puzzles per book)			
Vol. I: **Extracts** from the Bible	$7.95		
Vol. II: **Women** in the Bible	$7.95		
Vol. III: **Fathers** in the Bible	$7.95		
Vol. IV: **Prayers** in the Bible	$7.95		
Vol. V: **Victories** in the Bible	$7.95		
Vol. VI: **Parables** in the Bible	$7.95		
Vol. VII: **Promises** in the Bible	$7.95		
Vol. VIII: **Foundations** in Christianity (100 Puzzles)	$8.95		
Bible Word Search 8-Pack (all 8 books) - *17% off – Save $11.00*	$53.62		
Bible Word Search, **Large Print, No. 1**	$5.95		
Church Edition CD - *560 puzzles* – (7 volumes, lesson plans, group activities)	$5.95		
EDUCATOR'S WORD SEARCH Vol. 1: U.S. Presidents	$5.95		
Sub-Total			
NY Residents Add 8.5% Tax			
Shipping ($3.95 1st item, 50¢ each additional)			
TOTAL			

Date:_____ Payment: ⊡ Check ⊡ Money Order
Name:_____
Address:_____
City:_____ State:_____ Zip:_____
Telephone:_____
E-Mail:_____

www.ingramcontent.com/pod-product-compliance
Lightning Source LLC
Chambersburg PA
CBHW060443040426

42331CB00044B/2536